STUDIES IN AMERICAN LITERATURE

STUDIES IN AMERICAN LITERATURE

Volume XI

☆☆☆☆☆☆☆☆☆☆☆☆☆☆☆☆☆☆☆☆☆☆☆☆☆☆☆☆☆☆☆☆

THEMATIC DESIGN
IN
THE NOVELS OF
JOHN STEINBECK

by

LESTER JAY MARKS

Ohio University

1969
MOUTON

THE HAGUE · PARIS

LIBRARY OF CONGRESS CATALOG NUMBER: 68-24621

Printed in The Netherlands by Mouton & Co., Printers, The Hague

To the Memory of my Mother . . .
and to the Memory of
John Ernst Steinbeck: 1902 - 1968

ACKNOWLEDGEMENTS

I offer my gratitude to the many who have helped me with this study. To Professor David Owen, of Syracuse University, and Professor Eric Thompson, of Ohio University, who advised me. To Albert Serling, Warren Rubin, Ernest Johansson, and Professor Charles O'Donnell, who befriended me. To miss Elaine Gropper and Mr. Barry Leeds, Ohio University students who ably assisted in the preparation of the manuscript. To the librarians and aides at the libraries of Syracuse University and Ohio University, who cheerfully found what I sought. To Professor Edgar Whan, former Chairman of the Department of English at Ohio University, who gave me time and kindness. To my wife, who was all good things to me.

A grant from the Ohio University Research Committee helped make the publication of this book possible.

Acknowledgements are also due to the Viking Press, Inc., for permission to quote from the works of John Steinbeck, to the Rutgers University Press for quotations from Peter Lisca, *The Wide World of John Steinbeck*, and to The University of New Mexico Press for quotations from E. W. Tedlock Jr. and C. V. Wicker, ed., *Steinbeck and His Critics*.

L. J. M.

TABLE OF CONTENTS

INTRODUCTION

This book is concerned with the thematic design of the novels of John Steinbeck. Since most critical work on Steinbeck has tended to stress his wide variety of techniques and subject matter, the present study becomes particularly important in illustrating how a system of ideas exists beneath the surface diversities. These ideas may be seen to reside in three thematic patterns that recur consistently, though with unequal emphasis, throughout Steinbeck's novels.

The first of these patterns indicates that man is a religious creature and that each man creates a godhead to satisfy his personal religious need. The second pattern suggests that mankind may also be viewed biologically, as a "group animal" composed of individuals ("cells") but having a will and intelligence of its own, distinct from any one of its parts. However, outside the group is another kind of individual, analogous to the biologist himself, who, in the role of Steinbeck's constant hero, observes and comments upon the "animal". The final pattern in the thematic scheme illustrates the "non-teleological" concept that man lives without knowledge of the cause of his existence; nevertheless, the very mystery of life spurs his search for human values.

These themes will be considered not only as they embody Steinbeck's social, religious, and scientific "ideas", but also as they indicate his artistic vision and method — as they are *esthetically* resolved in his novels. First, however, before studying the novels textually, let us examine separately the nature and origin of each theme.

I

THREE THEMATIC PATTERNS

A PRIVATE RELIGION

Typical of John Steinbeck's fictional characters is their yearning for religious fulfilment. Critics, attempting to define and interpret this characteristic religious tendency, have come to widely differing conclusions. One critic, for example, believes that Steinbeck ultimately reduces man's devoutness to animalism, that Steinbeck "presents man as a captive ... of instincts and appetites only, blindly desiring and striving, not reasoning, judging, choosing but automatically responding to impulses and attractions".[1] Another, however, finds in *The Grapes of Wrath* "a contemporary adaptation of the Christ image" and indications of "some Christian meaning".[2] Still others have seen various of Steinbeck's characters as pagans, pantheists, transcendentalists, and animists. The revealing fact in all this critical diversity is that the particular arguments hold up rather well; a roll-call of Steinbeck's characters would indeed muster an army of separate creeds. I contend that this very variety of religious direction in his characters constitutes one of the important thematic patterns in Steinbeck's novels.

Although there seems to be no single term to describe the phenomenon of each man creating his private religion to conform to the dictates of his nature, there is reason to believe that such a phenomenon must have existed since man first sought an answer to

---

[1] John S. Kennedy, "John Steinbeck: Life Affirmed and Dissolved", *Steinbeck and His Critics*, ed. E. W. Tedlock and C. V. Wicker (Albuquerque, 1957), p. 127.
[2] Martin Staples Shockley, "Christian Symbolism in *The Grapes of Wrath*", *College English*, XVIII (November, 1956), 87.

the mystery of his being. Arguing for the existence of a universal religious propensity, George Santayana wrote:

Even the heretics and atheists, if they have profundity, turn out after a while to be forerunners of some new orthodoxy. What they rebel against is a religion alien to their nature; ... but they yearn mightily in their own souls after the religious acceptance of a world interpreted in their own fashion.[3]

And again: "Religion is an interpretation of the world, honestly made, and made in view of man's happiness and its empirical conditions."[4] Like Santayana, Steinbeck supposes that man is so constituted as to seek out a religion that suits his particular needs, and that if he finds none among those already existing, he creates his own.

I am not here attempting to prove "influences"; however, a further illustration of how Steinbeck's thinking is not without modern philosophical and psychological parallels will provide for the reader a few governing ideas, useful when we later examine Steinbeck's themes as they are embodied metaphorically in the novels. There are, for example, important similarities between Carl Jung's understanding of the role religion plays in man's life, and Steinbeck's theme of religious propensity, particularly as that theme is consistent with his "non-teleological" approach to life which I shall examine in greater detail later in this chapter. Jung, like Steinbeck, does not attribute man's religious sensibility to a series of observable causes; he insists that reductive methods cannot be used to *explain* the nature of the soul. Even when Jung affirms, in his theory of racial archetypes, that modern man's behavior patterns are traceable to his earliest history (and, in fact, to his animal ancestry), he denies that this knowledge of heritage in any way unveils the mystery of the existence of man's individual and collective souls. We can, in other words, know only that man has always thought, felt, and acted as he does now; we cannot know why. The word "spontaneously" is particularly significant in the following judgment from Jung:

[3] George Santayana, *The Life of Reason*, rev. ed. (New York, 1955), p. 179.
[4] *Ibid.*, p. 193.

Man has, everywhere and always, spontaneously developed religious forms of expression, and ... the human psyche from time immemorial has been shot through with religious feelings and ideas. Whoever cannot see this aspect of the human psyche is blind, and whoever chooses to explain it away, or to "enlighten" it away, has no sense of reality.[5]

Several passages from *Sea of Cortez*, Steinbeck's journal (with Edward Ricketts) of his scientific expedition into the Gulf of California, echo not only Jung's concept of archetypes, but even, at times, Jung's terminology. In the following example Steinbeck is speaking of the great "personal loss" that many of the people of Monterey would feel if scientists were to prove to them that the sea-monster they had seen was nothing more than a malformed sea-lion:

And the ocean would be none the better for it [the loss of the myth]. For the ocean, deep and black in the depths, is like the low dark levels of our minds in which the dream symbols incubate and sometimes rise up to sight like the Old Man of the Sea.....
We have thought often of this mass of sea-memory, or sea-thought, which lives deep in the mind. If one ask for a description of the unconscious, even the answer-symbol will usually be in terms of a dark water into which the light descends only a short distance. And we have thought how the human fetus has, at one stage of its development, vestigial gill-slits. If the gills are a component of the developing human, it is not unreasonable to suppose a parallel or concurrent mind or psyche development. If there be a life-memory strong enough to leave its symbol in vestigial gills, the preponderantly aquatic symbols in the individual unconscious might well be indications of a group psyche-memory which is the foundation of the whole unconscious.[6]

I shall discuss the further implications of the "group psyche-memory" in the second section of this chapter, but one may see in this passage a connection with Jung's concept of the religious aspect of the human psyche. In speaking of symbols ("the Old Man of the Sea") that have arisen from the depths of a collective unconscious, Steinbeck is helping to explain the tendency of his characters to choose symbols upon which they build their personal religions.

[5] Carl G. Jung, *Modern Man in Search of a Soul*, trans. W. S. Dill and Cary F. Baynes (New York, 1933), p. 140.
[6] John Steinbeck and Edward F. Ricketts, *Sea of Cortez* (New York, 1941), pp. 31-32.

In *The Wide World of John Steinbeck*, Peter Lisca commented briefly on this ritualizing tendency of the characters in *To A God Unknown* as it constituted their way of giving meaning to "situations beyond empirical control". Lisca saw the importance that

this novel places on man's unconscious heritage of the experiences of his race. This heritage is reflected in the characters' strange compulsions to engage in irrational rituals, and their susceptibility to symbols of whose significance they are not consciously aware. In later novels, this Jungian "race memory" is given a new dimension by Steinbeck's insights into marine biology.[7]

While Lisca recognizes Steinbeck's emphasis on ritual, he does not indicate how such "susceptibility to symbols" recurs through all the novels and how it is more than a kind of fetishism born of man's unconscious heritage. Indeed, no matter how much precedence we discover for this kind of symbol-making, and even if we find, with Steinbeck, that "the harvest of symbols in our minds seems to have been planted in the soft rich soil of our pre-humanity",[8] we are led to conclude that the *act* of creating ritual symbols (in effect the creation of a personal religion) is man's way (and the way of Steinbeck's characters) of providing order and meaning in his life. Man creates, in other words, a metaphor for what he could not otherwise know; he creates a metaphor for God.

THE GROUP ANIMAL AND ITS CELLS

Steinbeck's view of man as a religious being deals with the mind and with the soul of man and suggests a most romantic — perhaps sentimental — approach to life. Conversely, his group-animal theory deals with man (*en masse* and individually) as a biological creature and seems to imply that Steinbeck's approach to life is calculating and impersonal, that he is unconcerned with man's spiritual self. But Steinbeck is first of all an artist, and if his awareness of man as an animal seems incongruous with his aware-

---

[7] Peter Lisca, *The Wide World of John Steinbeck* (New Brunswick, 1958) pp. 53, 55.
[8] Steinbeck, p. 34.

ness of man's spirituality, both notions nevertheless have one important thing in common as Steinbeck employs them in his fiction: both work metaphorically to depict the artist's total vision of man's duality. For critical purposes each must be studied separately as *idea*, but as I shall show in the third of this three-pronged scheme, Steinbeck unites the two in a final moral and artistic resolution.

In an essay designed to show that metaphor "develops out of social conditions and in turn influences social behavior", Weller Embler concluded in part that while our age has found its "master metaphor" in the machine, "it is apparent that our contemporary social similitudes are often drawn from the biological sciences".[9] Embler's observations suggest how true a vision for our time is Steinbeck's theory and metaphor of the group animal. After alluding to Steinbeck's short story, "The Leader of the People", where westward-moving pioneers are "one big crawling beast", and wagons moving across the plains are "centipedes", Embler explains:

In Steinbeck's [search] for a social philosophy which could meet the problems of his day, he turned for assistance to the biological sciences. In these he found sound method, tested hypotheses, and, if it could be translated into language descriptive of human behavior, a body of usable information about subhuman life. ... And it became Steinbeck's habit to compare human beings with marine animals, with land animals, and with insects. It may be fairly said that Steinbeck's dramatic similarities between mice and men, between fish and men (*Sea of Cortez*), between centipedes and men, whether drawn from observation or embedded within the firm system of ecology, have changed the social thinking of many readers.[10]

And to this may be added that Steinbeck's group-animal metaphor, unlike machine metaphors (which imply futility), manages to convey a sense of the animal's conscious movement (implying hope).

In *Sea of Cortez* Steinbeck elaborates on the kind of observations that led to his group-man theory. Here he describes the activities of certain groups of primitive sea animals:

[9] Weller Embler, "Metaphor and Social Belief", *Etc.: A Review of General Semantics*, VIII (Winter, 1951), p. 92.
[10] *Ibid.*, p. 84.

There are colonies of pelagic tunicates which have taken a shape like the finger of a glove. Each member of the colony is an individual animal, but the colony is another individual animal, not at all like the sum of its individuals. Some of its colonists, girdling the open end, have developed the ability, one against the other, of making a pulsing movement very like muscular action. Others of the colonists collect the food and distribute it, and the outside of the glove is hardened and protected against contact. Here are two animals, and yet the same thing. ... [11]

Relating this activity to human behavior, Steinbeck maintains that the phenomenon must be regarded as a "mystery" in much the same sense as the early Church called something a mystery because it was not accessible to reason and simply had to be accepted "fully and deeply as *so*". Therefore,

a man of individualistic reason, if he must ask, "Which is the animal, the colony or the individual?" must abandon his particular kind of reason and say, "Why, it's two animals and they aren't alike any more than the cells of my body are like me. I am much more than the sum of my cells and, for all I know, they are much more than the division of me." There is no quietism in such acceptance, but rather the basis for a far deeper understanding of us and our world.[12]

Later in *Sea of Cortez*, referring to a school of fish, Steinbeck reinforces this idea of the group having an intelligence of its own and of each unit within the group having a special function:

And this larger animal, the school, seems to have a nature and drive and ends of its own. ... directed by a school intelligence. ... We suspect that when the school is studied as an animal rather than as a sum of unit fish, it will be found that certain units are assigned special functions to perform; that weaker or slower units may even take their place as placating food for the predators for the sake of the security of the school as an animal.[13]

We shall later see how Steinbeck consistently converts these ideas into analogies in his novels, but we need only remember the role played by the grandfather in "The Leader of the People" to understand the relative importance and special functions of units within the group. Without Grandfather, the leader, there would have been

[11] Steinbeck, p. 165.
[12] *Ibid.*
[13] *Ibid.*, pp. 240-241.

no direction, no *intelligent* movement for the "crawling beast". "The thing had to have a head", says Grandfather. And it also had to have men of skill — the gloved, muscular "hands" of Steinbeck's colony of sea animals. In "The Leader of the People", Billy Buck's grandfather, the mule-driver, is the man of skill who keeps the group in working condition while the leader directs its movements. In *The Grapes of Wrath*, Ma Joad heads the family group while Al keeps the old truck in repair; and in *In Dubious Battle*, Mac the Communist organizer is the "boss" who shows the worker, London, how to manipulate the strikers into a united force.

Curiously, none of these "units" within the group is Steinbeck's ultimate hero. We may love and respect Ma Joad, but she is bewildered, even in her persistent hope, by events she cannot control; we may admire Grandfather for having been a leader of people, but most of all we pity him for his lost strength; we may marvel at Mac's devotion to his cause and at his power, but we despise his brutal means to dubious ends. Always in Steinbeck's novels, however, is another figure who looms outside and above the group. Viewing the group with detached compassion is always Steinbeck's prototypical biologist-philosopher. As biologist he observes the "animal" with scientific objectivity, hoping to discover in its behavior an order and a meaning within an ecological framework. As philosopher, still concerned with order and meaning, but knowing that objective reality is only part of the truth, he frees himself of conventional scientific restrictions and allows himself the luxury of subjectivity; he views the group as men who, like himself, are spiritual beings seeking their place within a mysteriously ordered cosmos. But this hero is a character in his own right, and as a character he is loved, respected, feared, and misunderstood by the others. He is loved because he gives solace to the weak; he is respected because he lends himself to the causes of the group and helps to keep it alive; he is feared and misunderstood because he remains the outsider who never seems to wholly believe in the mundane causes of the group, and because his attitudes and methods transcend the group's understanding. Like the "good men most biologists are", Steinbeck writes in *Sea of Cortez*, he is "temperamental, moody, lecherous, loud-laughing, and healthy". But he also, as scientist, observes life, and he "learns something from it."[14]

As he appears in the novels, this hero may be, but is not always, a biologist by profession; but his attitudes and functions, as Steinbeck's hero type, remain consistent. He is Doc Burton in *In Dubious Battle*, "Doc" in *Cannery Row*, Jim Casy in *The Grapes of Wrath*, and Lee in *East of Eden*. Always, however, he is an outsider who speculates on the group from the biologist's non-teleological point of view. Finally, and perhaps most important, he is the metaphorical embodiment not only of Steinbeck's ideas but of his esthetic technique as well. Doc Burton illustrates this function when, in answer to Mac's concern over whether Doc really believes in the strikers' cause, he says:

Listen to me, Mac. My senses aren't above reproach, but they're all I have. I want to see the whole picture — as nearly as I can. I don't want to put on the blinders of "good" and "bad", and limit my vision. If I used the term "good" on a thing I'd lose my license to inspect it, because there might be bad in it. Don't you see? I want to be able to look at the whole thing.[15]

NON-TELEOLOGICAL THINKING AND A REVERENCE FOR LIFE

The third of Steinbeck's central idea-patterns arose out of his need to reconcile, philosophically and esthetically, his scientific approach to life with his view of man's essentially emotional religiousness. Several critics have concluded that this dichotomy in Steinbeck's thinking has been responsible for an important failure in his work — a failure to reconcile what Steinbeck called a "cold ... conscientious" observation with "human" elements.[16] Woodburn Ross, in "John Steinbeck: Earth and Stars", explained the problem this way:

Steinbeck's difficulty is that ... he is a man of two worlds. As a believer in the inductive, scientific method he must record what he sees, he must

[14] *Ibid.*, pp. 240-241.
[15] John Steinbeck, *In Dubious Battle* (New York, 1936), p. 143.
[16] Lisca, p. 115, cites Steinbeck's recognition of the problem in a letter from Steinbeck to his agents, McIntosh and Otis. Lisca is himself concerned with the dichotomy in regard to *In Dubious Battle*.

write realistically. But as a man of powerful affections and intuitions he must reflect irrational attitudes which are justifiable only in terms of the desires of the human spirit. He is therefore at the same time brutal and tender, rational and irrational, concrete and abstract. His imagination provides for humanity a home in the universe which his senses do not perceive.[17]

Ross concluded that Steinbeck, the irrationalist, finally wins out in the struggle with Steinbeck, the rationalist. I find, however, that no such mortal struggle existed for Steinbeck; instead, Steinbeck's "irrationalism", his reverence for the mysteries of life, is consistent with and in fact dependent upon his "rational", scientific methods — methods which result in what he calls "non-teleological" or "is" thinking. If Steinbeck is a "man of two worlds", we can be certain that Steinbeck the artist has dictated for those worlds a workable treaty of peace in words such as these:

Why do we so dread to think of our species as a species? Can it be that we are afraid of what we may find? That human self-love would suffer too much and that the image of God might prove to be a mask? This could be only partly true, for if we could cease to wear the image of a kindly, bearded, interstellar dictator, we might find ourselves true images of his kingdom, our eyes the nebulae, and universes in our cells.[18]

In *Sea of Cortez* Steinbeck details and defends his non-teleological methods. In the first place, he views *teleological* thinking as misleading and impractical:

What we personally conceive by the term "teleological thinking", ... is most frequently associated with the evaluating of causes and effects, the purposiveness of events. This kind of thinking considers changes and cures — what "should be" in the terms of an end pattern (which is often a subjective or anthropomorphic projection); it presumes the bettering of conditions, often, unfortunately, without achieving more than a most superficial understanding of those conditions. In their sometimes intolerant refusal to face facts as they are, teleological notions may substitute a fierce but ineffectual attempt to change conditions which are assumed to be undesirable, in place of the understanding-acceptance which would pave the way for a more sensible attempt at any change which might still be indicated.[19]

[17]   Woodburn O. Ross, "John Steinbeck: Earth and Stars", *The University of Missouri Studies*, XXI (1946), 187.
[18]   Steinbeck, *Sea of Cortez*, pp. 264-265.
[19]   *Ibid.*, pp. 134-135.

In this last sentence we can begin to see how Steinbeck does not preclude a kind of "change" taking place within the order of things "as they are". In fact, only by accepting things as they are can we understand them well enough to take "sensible" action. The limited nature of such change is implied in Steinbeck's following explanation of non-teleological thinking and in his allusion to Darwin:

Non-teleological ideas derive through "is" thinking, associated with natural selection as Darwin seems to have understood it. They imply depth, fundamentalism, and clarity — seeing beyond traditional or personal projections. They consider events as outgrowths and expressions rather than as results; conscious acceptance as a desideratum, and certainly as an all-important prerequisite. Nonteleological thinking concerns itself primarily not with what should be, or could be, or might be, but rather with what actually "is" — attempting at most to answer the already sufficiently difficult questions *what* or *how*, instead of *why*.[20]

So while teleological thinking may help us to see "relational aspects" of a whole picture, we should not be deceived into believing that it leads us to first cause. Events *occur* and changes take place (as in natural selection), but only dangerously wishful thinking lets us believe that we have the final answer to the question *why*. "The relational picture", Steinbeck continues, "should be regarded only as a glimpse — a challenge to consider also the rest of the relations as they are available — to envision the whole picture as well as can be done with given abilities and data."[21]

Steinbeck anticipates the horrified reactions to such non-causal thinking. He considers the fear of many people that the non-teleological approach would leave them "dangling out in space, deprived of such emotional support as had been afforded them by an unthinking belief ... in the institutions of tradition; religion; science; in the security of the home or the family; or in a comfortable bank account".[22] But he holds that this kind of thinking actually emancipates man from the trap he imposes upon himself by his "partial and biased mental reconstructings". Causal thinking leads man through a maze where at any blank wall he may stop and accept the illusion that he has finally reached the end. Non-

---

[20] *Ibid*., p. 135.
[21] *Ibid*., p. 142.
[22] *Ibid*., pp. 146-147.

teleological thinking recognizes the illusion for what it is and seeks
to understand the whole complex situation, thereby making way for
intelligent action. This is kinder, Steinbeck believes, than the false
security afforded by the illusion. Rather than cruelly depriving
man of his foundation for living,

non-teleological methods more than any other seem capable of great
tenderness, of an all-embracingness which is rare otherwise. Consider,
for instance, the fact that, once a given situation is deeply understood, no
apologies are required. There are ample difficulties even to understanding
conditions "as is". Once that has been accomplished, the "why" of it
(known now to be simply a relation, though probably a near and important one) seems no longer to be preponderantly important. It needn't
be condoned or extenuated, it just "is". It is seen merely as part of a more
or less dim whole picture. ... With the non-teleological treatment there
is only the love and understanding of instant acceptance; after that
fundamental has been achieved, the next step, if any should be necessary,
can be considered more sensibly.[23]

The "next step" for Steinbeck, after "instant acceptance", is just
such "all-embracingness" as comes from envisioning the "whole
picture". It is as if Steinbeck has taken one step beyond naturalism:
looking into the tide pool he discovers a particularly suitable
metaphor for man, but, as one critic perceived, "man is differentiat-
ed from the starfish by his ability to see his part, as well as play it.
Only men (though not all men) are able to achieve the understanding that 'man is related to the whole thing'."[24] Rather than
concluding that man is somehow diminished in stature because he
may be seen (individually and as a group) ecologically, as a cell in
a larger organism, Steinbeck assumes that man is ennobled by his
very awareness of his part in this whole great pattern. Out of
Steinbeck's biological investigation comes an attitude which, in its
reverence for the mystery of existence, can only be called religious.
In Steinbeck's explicit statement of philosophical discovery, one
may see how he progresses from biology to spirit and how, in fact,
he fuses the two:

[23] *Ibid.*
[24] Frederick Bracher, "Steinbeck and the Biological View of Man", *Steinbeck and His Critics*, ed. E. W. Tedlock and C. V. Wicker (Albuquerque, 1957), p. 196.

Our own interest lay in relationships of animal to animal. If one observes in this relational sense, it seems apparent that species are only commas in a sentence, that each species is at once the point and the base of a pyramid, that all life is relational to the point where an Einsteinian relativity seems to emerge. And then not only the meaning but the feeling grows misty. One merges into another, groups melt into ecological groups until the time when what we know as life meets and enters what we think of as non-life; barnacle and rock, rock and earth, earth and tree, tree and rain and air. And the units nestle into the whole and are inseparable from it. Then one can come back to the microscope and the tide pool and the aquarium. But the little animals are found to be changed, no longer set apart and alone.

And then the *fusion* of biology and spirit:

And it is a strange thing that most of the feeling we call religious, most of the mystical outcrying which is one of the most prized and used and desired reactions of our species, is really the understanding and the attempt to say that man is related to the whole thing, related inextricably to all reality, known and unknowable. This is a simple thing to say, but the profound feeling of it made a Jesus, a St. Augustine, a St. Francis, a Roger Bacon, a Charles Darwin, and an Einstein. Each of them in his own tempo and with his own voice discovered and reaffirmed with astonishment the knowledge that all things are one thing and that one thing is all things — plankton, a shimmering phosphorescence on the sea and the spinning planets and an expanding universe, all bound together by the elastic string of time. It is advisable to look from the tide pool to the stars and then back to the tide pool again.[25]

In the hope that the reader might see how Steinbeck intends his non-teleological methods to work for him both scientifically and philosophically, I have alluded often in this section to his expository writing in *Sea of Cortez*. But perhaps most important, as I indicated in my discussion of Steinbeck's views on religion and the group man, is the application of his ideas to his esthetic techniques. In the first pages of *Sea of Cortez* Steinbeck writes of the need for such application, and then, in illustration, tells of the non-teleological "design" of his book:

The design of a book is the pattern of reality controlled and shaped by the mind of the writer. This is completely understood about poetry or fiction, but is too seldom realized about books of fact. ... We have a book

[25]   Steinbeck, *Sea of Cortez*, pp. 216-217.

to write about the Gulf of California. We could do one of several things about its design. But we have decided to let it form itself: its boundaries a boat and a sea; its duration a six weeks' charter time; its subject everything we could see and think and even imagine; its limits — our own without reservation. ... We wanted to see everything our eyes would accommodate, to think what we could, and, out of our seeing and thinking, to build some kind of structure in modeled imitation of the observed reality.[26]

Here then, Steinbeck is saying to his readers, is what happened, perceptually and conceptually; no explanations are needed — these things just happened. But Steinbeck, as the artist must, reserves the right of selection and emphasis; in a word, the right to *order* the "pattern of reality". "This trip", Steinbeck writes at the conclusion of his book, "had dimension and tone. ... Some creative thing had happened."[27]

Indeed, the same kind of creative thing happens in Steinbeck's novels as happened in *Sea of Cortez*. The characters of his novels are compelled, by what they unexplainably *are*, to choose personal religious rituals and symbols that give meaning to their existence. In their symbol-making activities, such characters become an essential part of Steinbeck's non-teleological world of the novel; what they accomplish (not always by conscious method) is an awareness of what they are, which includes an acknowledgement of irrationality as well as rationality. Now, having seen themselves in the tide pool, they look to the stars and make the attempt, through symbol and ritual, to relate themselves to "the whole thing ..., to all reality, known and unknowable".

I have noted how Steinbeck, consistent with his non-teleological methods, also creates in his novels a metaphorical group animal composed of individual cells, each cell with a life of its own. In this scheme, after he has given them individual spiritual identification, Steinbeck enables his characters to join themselves, as if *biologically*, to a greater reality — to the group itself. While the phenomenon (the *why*) of the group animal remains a "mystery", the individual may perceive that as a part of the group he is "like" it, and yet that he is important as an individual within it. He finds

26   *Ibid.*, pp. 1-2.
27   *Ibid.*, p. 270.

identity as an individual and, by projection, as a part of the whole physical pattern of the universe. Still, the individual's view is limited to his own place in the whole pattern. Hence Steinbeck creates his biologist-hero who applies Steinbeck's non-teleological methods of observation to the several complex relationships and, acting as a kind of chorus, comments on the whole picture.

Steinbeck's third idea-pattern, as I have indicated, consists of a fusion of his views of man as a physical and as a spiritual being. Although a belief in the unity of all things is not new, one critic has suggested that Steinbeck is "the first significant novelist to begin to build a mystical religion upon a naturalistic base".[28] I do not believe, however, that Steinbeck's conclusions are any more "mystical" than, as Steinbeck himself pointed out, those reached by Darwin, Einstein, or Emerson, all of whom went to the physical world, the world of matter, and found that man in nature was a microcosm of a greater design. What is perhaps unique with Steinbeck is his application of non-teleological methods to his novels; and, since his central metaphor, in keeping with his philosophical beliefs, is biological, an esthetic technique along the same scientific lines follows naturally. With his biological point of view Steinbeck perceived a certain order in nature, and he found that, as an artist, he could recreate those perceptions in metaphorical terms that had meaning for humanity. Edmund Sinnott, who defined "spirit" as "the highest expressions of biological goal-seeking", paralleled much of Steinbeck's thinking when he wrote:

In nature there is a Principle of Organization which, through life, brings order out of chaos, spirit out of matter, and personality out of impersonal stuff. ... Life, manifest in organisms, is integrating, purposeful, and creative. We cannot yet explain these qualities, but through them we may gain a clearer spiritual insight into man's nature and his relation to the universe than through intellect alone.[29]

Steinbeck's novels attempt to create just such a Principle of Organization in what he has called "modeled imitation of the observed reality". Steinbeck's artistic method, then, reflecting his

[28]   Woodburn O. Ross, "John Steinbeck: Naturalism's Priest", *College English*, X (May, 1949), p. 438.
[29]   Edmund W. Sinnott, *The Biology of the Spirit* (New York, 1955), pp. 122-123.

non-teleological method, is to create a series of relational events that *happened*. His novels do not say what *should be* but only what *is*. But the reader is enabled by this method to see the intrinsic order of life within the novel, and is further enabled to perceive how this order is at once a reflection of and is inseparable from the nature of all things. Man in Steinbeck's novels is ennobled, first by accepting the mystery of his existence and then by seeking to discover his place in the universal scheme.

II

CUP OF GOLD

Cup of Gold was first published in 1929 and republished in 1936 after Steinbeck had earned a literary reputation with *Tortilla Flat*. Even then, however, it was given little critical attention, and some critics still regard it as the abortive first creation of an inexperienced writer. But the fact is that Steinbeck had written and destroyed two earlier novels and had rewritten *Cup of Gold* six times before it was published. The novel does fail, but not for lack of experience or serious purpose on Steinbeck's part; rather, it fails because of its tonal inconsistencies — its unwarranted shifts from tragedy to melodrama to farce. One wonders whether the novel's subtitle, *A Life of Sir Henry Morgan, Buccaneer, with Occasional Reference to History*, was perhaps added as a facetious afterthought when Steinbeck saw how his good intentions had gone astray.

The plot of the novel, as Peter Lisca points out, has "all the requirements of a Hollywood historical extravaganza", but Lisca also believes that Steinbeck ambitiously took the Faust legend for his theme, "especially as adapted in some form or other by Hawthorne for almost every one of his works", and took the quest for the Holy Grail as a subsidiary theme.[1] Perhaps. But since Morgan's plight becomes comic and Morgan himself becomes pathetic, it appears to me that Morgan can be neither a Chillingworth nor a Galahad. Nevertheless, Steinbeck meant to create, in Morgan, a character of tragic stature, one who is fated from birth to become great as a leader of men but who is corrupted by a growing obsession for power which isolates him from mankind.

[1] Peter Lisca, *The Wide World of John Steinbeck* (New Brunswick, 1958), pp. 26-31.

Unfortunately, Henry Morgan the boy, who yearns for "the moon to drink from as a golden cup", and for whom the local bard prophesies greatness — "'In time you will be alone in your greatness and no friend anywhere; only those who hold you in respect or fear or awe'"[2] — never becomes a man of awesome quality. He becomes instead a self-deceiving liar and a pathetic fop. For example, as a farmer's son in Wales Henry is infatuated with a cottager's daughter, but when he leaves to go adventuring he still has not overcome his boyish shyness enough even to speak to her. Year after year, as his fame spreads and the list of his tyrannies grows, Morgan, we perceive, has no great dream but only an adolescent illusion of romantic love kept alive by the constant embellishment of his imagination. Finally when Morgan, having bought a pardon and knighthood, "lumpish" and mired in a loveless marriage of his middle years, tells the story of his childhood romance to King Charles, he distorts it ridiculously and the reader knows him for a fool. He half believes that he was the son of a gentleman and that the cottager's daughter was "a little princess of France" who, as he tells it, would have fled with him had not her father's soldiers separated them and caused her, in her misery, to poison herself.

The bard had also told young Henry that "all the world's great have been little boys who wanted the moon", that Henry would become great if he remained a child. This idea is repeated often in the story, and we are asked to believe that it is a good thing representing a youthful spirit of adventure, innocent courage, and high moral aspirations. But there is a serious inconsistency between what is *said* of Henry's child-like virtues and the kind of immature weaknesses which he actually embodies. Assuming that the great man becomes great because of his restlessness combined with an innocent view of his purpose, and that he falls when he comes to see his weaknesses, Steinbeck had hoped to create Morgan with tragic proportions. But he produced only a bully who is puzzled when time leaves him bereft of power to frighten and alone with sentimental memories and illusions. The trouble with Steinbeck's Henry Morgan is that, while he is meant to be a man gifted with a

[2] John Steinbeck, *Cup of Gold* (New York, 1929), p. 28.

child's pure vision, he is never more than a boy with infantile daydreams.

When *Cup of Gold* was republished, Steinbeck wrote to his agents that he was "not particularly proud" of the book and wished "it had never been published".[3] Nevertheless, *Cup of Gold* is important because it convinced him, fortunately, to turn from the historical novel to places and people familiar to him, and because it indicates, in embryo, several of Steinbeck's developing themes. For example, Henry Morgan's failure to rise above his illusions, his narrow egocentricity, foreshadows the pattern of Steinbeck's leader type, his men of action of the novels that followed. But more important, Morgan's deterioration as a heroic figure suggests that Steinbeck had no real faith in Morgan's kind of fame or in his search for power. After *Cup of Gold*, the Morgans take a secondary position as narrow-visioned men of earth-bound ideals, while another type, skeptical of power and ever struggling to see life whole, emerges as Steinbeck's hero.

As I pointed out in my first chapter, Steinbeck's typical leader, the "head" of his group animal, is motivated by his dedication to a cause. The leader may be a sympathetic character with a nobly inspired cause, as Ma Joad in her struggle to keep the family together; he may be pitifully bound by habit and tradition to the cause of evil, as Colonel Lanser in *The Moon is Down*; or he may lose sight of his original purpose and dedicate himself to power for its own sake, as Henry Morgan in *Cup of Gold*. In all cases, despite their penchant for careful planning, Steinbeck's leaders always fail to gain final victories; the reason is their narrow vision. The difference between Henry Morgan and, for example, Mac in *In Dubious Battle*, also a leader of a lost cause, lies in Steinbeck's unsuccessful attempt to make Morgan his hero, whereas Mac is intentionally relegated to an inferior role to make way for Doc Burton, who searches beyond mundane creeds in order to see the larger picture.

Even in *Cup of Gold*, however, there is one character who clearly foreshadows the biologist-hero of the later novels. Coeur de Gris,

---

[3] Cited by Lewis Gannett in "John Steinbeck's Way of Writing", the Introduction to *The Portable Steinbeck* (New York, 1946), p. viii.

Morgan's lieutenant on their long march to capture the city of Panama (known as the Cup of Gold), is a constant witness to Morgan's egotism and self-deception. On one occasion he confronts Morgan with the real reason that Morgan wants to take Panama: a lust to capture the woman there who has become a legend for her beauty and a symbol of what all men seek. But for Morgan (still a boy-man) this woman is a projection of the girl he was too shy to approach years before in Wales. Coeur de Gris does not know this, but he does perceive how Morgan's adventures and fame are based upon shallow rather than noble motives, and he is not deceived (as are the armies which follow Morgan) into believing that Morgan is the leader of some great crusade. When Morgan boasts, god-like, of the inner yearnings and ambitions that make him great, adding that other men cannot understand them, Coeur de Gris scornfully cries out:

"Do you think I do not understand? I know; to your mind your feelings are new things, discoveries of fresh importance. Your failures are un-precedented. This gigantic conceit will not allow you to believe that this Cockney behind you [one of the soldiers] — yes, he who sometimes rolls on the ground in fits — might have the same hopes and despairs as your-self. You cannot believe that these men feel as deeply as you do. ..."
    Captain Morgan had flushed under the lash of words. He did not believe it. It was monstrous to think that these men could feel as he did. Such a comparison made him, somehow, unworthy.[4]

Another indication of Coeur de Gris as an embryonic Steinbeck hero, is his ability to see Morgan's weaknesses even while he continues to understand Morgan and pity him for his illusions. Coeur de Gris seems to face the truth in much the same way as does Doc Burton, yet both men have no faith in the expeditions with which they have linked themselves: Doc does not believe that the strikers will win out over the owners, and Coeur de Gris knows that capturing Panama will be a hollow victory. Just as Mac questions Doc about why he remains if he does not believe in the cause, so Morgan asks what Coeur de Gris hopes to gain, and Coeur de Gris answers: "'I expect to find nothing.'" It is simply Coeur de Gris' compassion for man in his folly, and his desire to come ever

4 Steinbeck, Cup of Gold, p. 176.

closer to a sight of life's total meaning, that sustains his loyalty to Morgan and to mankind. And though Coeur de Gris is never as fully developed as Doc Burton as a spokesman for Steinbeck, his insight into the universality of man's struggles, illusions and failures is echoed in Doc's words:

"There aren't any beginnings. ... Nor any ends. It seems to me that man has engaged in a blind and fearful struggle out of a past he can't remember, into a future he can't foresee nor understand. And man has met and defeated every obstacle, every enemy except one. He cannot win over himself."[5]

Although *Sea of Cortez* was not to be written for another twelve years, *Cup of Gold* offers ample evidence that Steinbeck's concepts of the "leader of men" and the "observing biologist" were developing parallel to his scientific viewpoint and his metaphor of the group animal. To explain young Morgan's wistful yearning to wander, Steinbeck employs the image of a flock of birds: "Perhaps the same force moved him which collected the birds into exploring parties and made the animals sniff up-wind for the scent of winter."[6] Later in the story, as Morgan's army treks towards Panama, Steinbeck describes the army as if it were an insect trying to get by an obstacle: "At a command, the head of the wriggling column swung to the left and began to gnaw its way through the thicker underbrush."[7] And when the captain of Panama's army proudly views his troops, "following his orders as though they were the multimembers of one great body governed by his brain",[8] his attitude is markedly similar to Mac's, in *In Dubious Battle*, when Mac speaks of his mob of strikers as an animal, with himself as its head to give it direction: "People think a mob is wasteful, but I've seen plenty; and I tell you, a mob with something it wants to do is just about as efficient as trained soldiers."[9] Although Mac and Morgan are leaders, their egotism narrows their imagination. Doc Burton and Coeur de Gris, on the other hand, are not "men of action" and, thus

---

[5]   John Steinbeck, *In Dubious Battle* (New York, 1936), p. 253.
[6]   Steinbeck, *Cup of Gold*, p. 5.
[7]   *Ibid.*, p. 179.
[8]   *Ibid.*, p. 183.
[9]   Steinbeck, *In Dubious Battle*, p. 316.

alienated from the group, they are capable of viewing it whole and of passing judgment upon it.

The narrowness of Henry Morgan's understanding of his own life, and the illusions he manufactures to avoid seeing the truth, suggest still another of the themes which were to become important in Steinbeck's later novels: the reverence for life that arises out of non-teleological thinking. According to Steinbeck's theory, Morgan was doomed to pathetic failure because of his self-centered belief that his action would make great changes in the world, an attitude that Steinbeck termed "teleological". As I noted earlier (see above, p. 20), Steinbeck believed that this kind of thinking "considers changes and cures — what 'should be' ... ; it presumes the bettering of conditions, often unfortunately, without achieving more than a most superficial understanding of those conditions. In their sometimes intolerant refusal to face facts as they are, teleological notions may substitute a fierce but ineffectual attempt to change conditions." Morgan, who "wanted the moon", is the first of the long line of Steinbeck's characters who dream of "what should be" but fail to see "what is". Describing Morgan's desires as essentially selfish, Frederick I. Carpenter wrote of Morgan's failure:

> The world's great who have dreamed only of personal power, and have sought to achieve it only through violence, have always failed ultimately. So this Henry Morgan failed in love and happiness: although he achieved his dream of power through violence, it did him little good.[10]

As long as Morgan dreams of power, he will remain tied to the illusion that he can "change conditions". One character in *Cup of Gold* makes a significant judgment of Morgan when he observes that "folly and distorted vision are the foundations of greatness".[11] But "greatness" is here synonymous with worldly success gained at the sacrifice of the kind of clear vision that made Coeur de Gris wiser than Morgan.

Steinbeck wrote that non-teleological ideas "imply depth, fundamentalism, and clarity — seeing beyond traditional or personal projections" in an attempt to see what is. (see above, p. 21)

[10]   Frederick I. Carpenter, "John Steinbeck: American Dreamer", *Southwest Review*, XXVI (July, 1941), 457.
[11]   Steinbeck, *Cup of Gold*, p. 250.

Obviously, Morgan's inability to see his power and fame as fraudulent illusions is what makes him, for the reader, a fool. Out of fear that his position as leader will be questioned, Morgan refuses to believe that he is like other men; typical of Steinbeck's leaders, his narrow vision raises him to the unenviable position at the head of causes destined to be lost.

In *Cup of Gold* Steinbeck began to shape, however crudely, the thematic patterns of his later novels. After this first novel, the themes did not suddenly appear full-blown or in neat relationship. But his handling of some of them, even in his second novel, indicates a substantial advance in his knowledge of his intentions and in his ability as an artist.

III

TO A GOD UNKNOWN: THE YEARNING FOR RITUAL

Seeking to understand the "curious compromise" between naturalism and mysticism in Steinbeck's work, Woodburn Ross first of all
acknowledges Steinbeck's position that "humanity is a product of
natural forces and [that] ... the profoundest biological urge is the
urge for life".[1] Ross then notes how Steinbeck transcends the
natural world of perceptual experience:

> Now much of Steinbeck's basic position is essentially religious, though
> not in any orthodox sense of the word. In his very love of nature he
> assumes an attitude characteristic of mystics. He is religious in that he
> contemplates man's relation to the cosmos and attempts, although
> perhaps fumblingly, to understand it. He is religious in that he seeks to
> transcend scientific explanations based upon sense experience. He is
> religious in that from time to time he explicitly attests the holiness of
> nature. ... Steinbeck even finds holiness in "natural" conduct which,
> measured by conventional standards, would be found immoral.[2]

In Steinbeck's second novel, *To A God Unknown,* still a prelude to
later work where his three important thematic patterns were to
blend, we may find the greatest implicit concentration of his concept of man as a religious being.

Steinbeck's two sources for the title of the book, and the liberties
he took in altering them to suit his own purposes, are clear sign-
posts to the novel's central theme. The first of these sources, which
Steinbeck also used as the book's epigraph, is a poem from the
Rigveda which praises the "God over Gods" and invokes His
mercy through the offering of a sacrifice. As Peter Lisca points

---

[1] Woodburn O. Ross, "John Steinbeck: Naturalism's Priest", *College English,*
X (May, 1949), 433.
[2] *Ibid.,* pp. 436-437.

out,[3] Steinbeck omitted the first and last stanzas of the original and changed the rhythm to resemble that of the psalms (a rhythm called upon often throughout the book as a device to sustain a tone of supplication). More important, however, are Steinbeck's alterations of the poem's title and last lines in order to effect a new meaning. The original is known as the "Hymn to *the* Unknown God". (Italics mine.) There is nothing in this title, nor in the poem itself, to suggest any doubt as to the identity or the power of the God referred to; He is the Creator of all things, the "God over Gods". He is called "unknown" only because of His omniscience; that is, man's knowledge is diminutive compared to His, and His will is unquestionable. The line, "May He not injure us, Who is the begetter of earth ... ", is a prayerful invocation and an *affirmation* of supremacy. But Steinbeck turns this line into a question: "May he not hurt us, He who made earth, / Who made the sky and the shining sea?" and thereby prepares us for the god or gods of the novel, whose nature is *sought* but not immediately known.

The refrain of Steinbeck's version of the poem is also a question: "Who is the God to whom we shall offer sacrifice?" This and Steinbeck's title, "To a God Unknown", suggest, first of all, that there could be many gods and, further, that the one supreme God (to whom we shall sacrifice), is not readily identified. *The* God of the original poem is identifiable and universal; on the other hand, the god Steinbeck fashions is not only unpredictable (and hence *unknowable*), but is also unknown because he is unseen; he must first be discovered if he is to be offered sacrifice — a point, we shall see, that is central to the novel.

Steinbeck also changed the letter and spirit of the second source of his title. In Acts, XVII, of the Bible, Paul chastises the Athenians for their superstitions:

For as I passed by, and beheld your devotions, I found an altar with this inscription, TO THE UNKNOWN GOD. Whom therefore ye ignorantly worship, him declare I unto you.

Paul goes on to preach that God is one and "dwelleth not in tem-

---

[3]   Peter Lisca, *The Wide World of John Steinbeck* (New Brunswick, 1958), pp. 41-43.

ples" but in heaven, and that men do wrong who worship graven images. Again, Steinbeck's title is evidence, borne out by the events of the novel, that he rather favored the paganism of the Athenians to Paul's dogmatism. In fact, though there are no out and out villains in the book, the novel's least sympathetic character kills the joy of living for others by preaching, much like Paul, against the "sinfulness" of their pagan rituals. The hero of the novel, himself inclined towards fetishism, recognizes the right of each man to worship according to the needs of his own soul; proselytizing, he believes, is therefore futile and objectionable. Warned of the wrath of God that comes to idolators, he replies: "'Don't interfere with my games. Keep to your own.'"[4] *To A God Unknown* easily evidences Steinbeck's view of man as a religious creature, but more important in the novel is the nature of the individual's search for an answer to the question, "Who is He to whom we shall offer our sacrifice?" And each character, after searching in his own way, provides an answer that fulfils the yearning of his soul; each creates a private religion with uniquely personal rituals to satisfy the god or gods he has discovered.

The plot, though simple, also involves a search: Joseph Wayne leaves his Vermont farm to seek new land as a homesteader in California. He settles in the fertile valley of Nuestra Senora and, after learning of his father's death, sends for his brothers and their families. Together, with Joseph as the acknowledged head of the colony, they prosper until a drought impoverishes the land and forces them to move. But Joseph has developed a mystical attachment to the land and remains behind to offer himself as a sacrifice in desperate hope that his act will bring rain.

Part of the book is concerned with people restlessly moving westward in search of a place to belong to, a kind of happy valley that has long been a popular trademark for Steinbeck as a result of such works as *The Pastures of Heaven*, "The Leader of the People", *Of Mice and Men*, and *The Grapes of Wrath*. But *To A God Unknown*, as certainly as the other books, is after more fertile meanings than just those implied by the longing of displaced Americans for domestic security. Indeed, the story itself is but one of the devices,

[4]   John Steinbeck, *To A God Unknown* (New York, 1933), p. 172.

within a complex technique, that leads the reader to the far more important search of the human soul for its place in the universal scheme of things. Steinbeck found this mystical theme difficult to set forth without its becoming banal and sentimental, without its preternatural aspects becoming merely bizarre; but Steinbeck does succeed in making characters and events believable even while they are symbols of men's souls on their separate pilgrimages.

The tone of a religious pilgrimage is set in the novel's first chapter when Joseph Wayne's ancient father, passing the patriarchy to his son, gives Joseph leave to seek land in the west:

"You're not the oldest, Joseph, but I've always thought of you as the one to have the blessing. Thomas and Burton are good men, good sons, but I've always intended the blessing for you, so you could take my place. ... There's something more strong in you than in your brothers, Joseph; more sure and inward."[5]

And although Joseph is not alone in the novel as a seeker after unknown gods, his inherited position as family patriarch, and the way in which he comes to regard himself as a priest of the land (responsible for its fertility through his oblations), make his search a symbolic focal point. Even his entrance into the valley is somehow made to sound momentous and fateful in its parable-like intonation: "After a time of wandering, Joseph came to the long valley called Nuestra Senora, and there he recorded his homestead."[6] Almost immediately Joseph's mystical relation to the land begins to take shape:

There was a curious femaleness about the interlacing boughs and twigs, about the long green cavern cut by the river through the trees and the brilliant underbrush. The endless green halls and aisles and alcoves seemed to have meanings as obscure and promising as the symbols of an ancient religion.[7]

This fusion of female sexual imagery with the image of a cathedral indicates to Joseph that the land is holy and that he must make it fruitful. A few pages later, again as the land's "priest", he symbolically consummates a marriage to it:

[5] *Ibid.*, p. 3.
[6] *Ibid.*, p. 6.
[7] *Ibid.*, p. 8.

He stamped his feet into the soft earth. Then the exultance grew to be a sharp pain of desire that ran through his body in a hot river. He flung himself face downward on the grass and pressed his cheek against the wet stems. His fingers gripped the wet grass and tore it out, and gripped again. His thighs beat heavily on the earth. ... For a moment the land had been his wife.[8]

Joseph also discovers that the land has a "heart". He is led by an Indian friend, Juanito, to a quiet glade where a stream runs out of the side of a huge rock shaped "something like an altar". Joseph senses why the Indians regard the place as sacred, why their pregnant women, for example, come there to ponder the mystery of the new life within them — as Joseph's own young wife is later to be drawn to the glade. " 'This is ancient — and holy' ", Joseph says, trying to pacify the fears of his brother Tom. " 'There's something strong and sweet and good in there. There's something like food in there, and like cool water. ... Maybe sometime when we have need, we'll go back again — and be fed.' "[9] Here is the fountainhead, and it is to this place, when the stream seems about to dry up from the drought, that Joseph comes to nourish the earth with his own blood, to return himself to the earth so that the cycle of life may continue.

While these passages indicate Steinbeck's great passion for the mysteries of the wilderness, they are not the kind of call for a return of civilization to the old, primitive gods of Nature that one might expect to find, say, in D. H. Lawrence. There are, in fact, as I shall soon show, other gods and other religions in this book equally as valid for their adherents as Joseph's beliefs are for him. But Steinbeck is trying to show, quite consistent with his growing biological view of man, that man in his search for ritual cannot easily ignore the fact that he is in and of the self-perpetuating cycle of Nature. When Joseph enters the glade for the first time but remembers having seen it before, "perhaps in an old dream", he is symbolizing the primitive heritage of man's affinity to Nature — what Steinbeck called a "psyche memory".

Steinbeck's theme of man's universal religious propensity takes

8   *Ibid.*, p. 14.
9   *Ibid.*, pp. 56-57.

its complexity from his characters' diverse ritualism as they seek personal gods. Though Nature is always the catalyst, men react to it diversely. Joseph, his three brothers, his wife Elizabeth, his sister-in-law, the local priest Father Angelo, and an old hermit — all choose separate ways to search for their places in the mysterious unity in the universe.

Though Joseph seeks his way through pagan rites, they are curiously blended with pantheism and ancestor worship. Joseph's "kinship" (a word Steinbeck uses frequently to link characters to their respective objects of worship) is with the land, and, as we have seen, his ultimate sacrifice is to his symbol for its "heart" (the rock), and to its "blood-stream" (the spring), in the glade. But an even more personal symbol for Joseph, and the object for his everyday oblations, is the great oak tree next to which, because he felt that the spirit of his dead father had come to reside in the tree, he built his house. At first, suspicious and a little embarrassed by his feelings, he merely speaks to the tree. But gradually his faith grows, and to "work against" the return of the dry years to the land he hangs on the oak tree dead hawks and he nails to it the notchings of calves' ears. Questioned by his brother Thomas, Joseph replies:

"Maybe you can figure it out. I just do the things I do, I don't know why except that it makes me happy to do them. After all ... , a man has to have something to tie to, something he can trust to be there in the morning."[10]

Joseph's actions represent sacrifices to both the land and his father's spirit; as the multi-symbol for Father-god and Nature-god, the tree provides Joseph with his answer to the question, "Who is the God to whom we shall offer sacrifice?" His actions are irrational (and he knows it) but they make him "happy". Earlier in the novel Joseph had for the same reason approved of Juanito's claim to Castillian ancestry — the belief harmed nobody and it made Juanito happy to think of himself as a Castillian. In fact, Joseph offered, "'My father thinks he is almost a god. And he is.'"[11]

10   *Ibid.*, p. 52.
11   *Ibid.*, p. 20.

Through the tree, therefore, Joseph enables himself to worship his father (the patriarch) and the earth (perpetual woman). Joseph, the reader will recall, has had patriarchal authority passed down to him, and his responsibility as the new patriarch is to the land, to keep it fertile. His ancestral heritage, we may now see, is necessarily one with the kinship he feels for the land: His "was the heritage of a race which for a million years had sucked at the breasts of the soil and cohabited with the earth".[12]

Joseph's brother Burton, an austere and pietistic Protestant, is the antithesis of Joseph. He "was one whom *nature* had constituted for a [sectarian] religious life. . .' Celibacy was a *natural* state for him".[13] (Italics mine.) Burton is compulsively concerned with "sin" and hopes to appease his god and to cleanse his soul through suffering:

Burton was never well. His cheeks were drawn and lean, and his eyes hungry for a pleasure he did not expect this side of heaven. In a way it gratified him that his health was bad, for it proved that God thought of him enough to make him suffer.[14]

Unfortunately for the other characters, Burton sees evil all about him and feels morally obligated to aid in their salvation by showing them the way to suffering (and sometimes by inducing it.) He had embraced his wife only four times, vigorously protecting her from sins of the flesh and ruling her

with a firm and scriptural hand. He parceled out his thoughts to her and pared down her emotions when they got out of line. He knew when she exceeded the laws, and when, as happened now and then, some weak thing in Harriet cracked and left her sick and delirious, Burton prayed beside her bed until her mouth grew firm again and stopped its babbling.[15]

Steinbeck does not, in Burton, symbolize all Christian orthodoxy. Indeed, some of Steinbeck's best fictional friends are sectarian Christians, and even in this novel Father Angelo is nearly as much of a hero as Joseph. But Burton does represent a sort of joyless puritanism, and his narrow vision in damning those who find moral

[12] *Ibid.*, p. 42.
[13] *Ibid.*, p. 38.
[14] *Ibid.*
[15] *Ibid.*

good through their senses and in the physical world, makes him Joseph's spiritual and intellectual antagonist. Although Joseph tolerates and even respects Burton's code, alien as it is to Joseph, Burton hates and fears any but his own. He is found "whimpering and praying" in protest against the ritual dancing of the Mexicans and the mass held by Father Angelo: "'It's devil-worship, I tell you! On our own place! First the devil-worshiping priest and his wooden idols, and then this [dancing].'"[16] Ironically, Burton's praying falls into the rhythm of the guitars, as if even he cannot entirely purge himself of his primitive heritage.

Burton's god is essentially anthropomorphic: it is therefore Burton's own sense of sin that he responds to when he answers his god's call for retribution upon idolators. When Joseph wants to put his infant son in the "arms" of the oak tree, Burton warns him that "'a thing like this will not go unpunished'". But Joseph sees no sin in the act, although he understands that "'if Burton were doing what I am, it would be sin'".[17] And similarly, when Burton expresses shock over Joseph's passionately urging a bull to mount a cow ("'I want the land to swarm with life'"), Joseph's thoughts imply the inherent difference between the two brothers: "'He has a secret in him that makes everything I think or do unclean. I have heard the telling of the secret and it means nothing to me.'"[18] At the heart of the difference is the fact that Joseph, with pride in himself as a priest of Nature, equates good with fertility and evil with barrenness, while Burton finds Nature obscene because it seems in its creative processes to mock his celibacy and his sterile asceticism. Burton finally leaves the farm to seek a more compatible setting in a religious community, but before he leaves he spitefully kills Joseph's tree.

Thomas, the third of the Wayne brothers, is an idealized version of man as an animal. He seems at times to be a symbol of the unadulterated life of the instinct, and Steinbeck uses him as a norm to measure in the other characters the extent and kind of their variation from the primitive. Because he is mindless, he is free of

[16]   *Ibid.*, p. 162.
[17]   *Ibid.*, p. 207.
[18]   *Ibid.*, pp. 44-45.

the conflicts of rational men at war with themselves and the world. His code, if indeed it may be called such, is one with the struggle for survival; his "kinship" is with all animals:

He was not kind to animals; at least no kinder than they were to each other, but he must have acted with a consistency beasts could understand, for all creatures trusted him. ... Thomas liked animals and understood them, and he killed them with no more feeling than they had about killing each other. He was too much an animal himself to be sentimental.[19]

As for humans, Thomas shied from them, distrusting and frightened by their ways. "'You are afraid of every kind of ritual'", Joseph says to him, "'Do you know why?'" And Thomas answers, "'No, I don't know why ... , it seems a trap, a kind of little trap.'"[20]

Steinbeck's novels often include characters who live close to the level of animals and who, like Thomas, are more important as symbols of the primitive instincts that abide in all men than as "realistic" flesh and blood people; for example, Lennie in *Of Mice and Men*, the Pirate in *Tortilla Flat*, Grampa in *The Grapes of Wrath* — all fit into the pattern. And though Steinbeck is always sympathetic to these characters, always a little nostalgic about the sweetness of their innocence, he invariably emphasizes their symbolic position as free agents (free because of their mindlessness) in an ideally unfettered world that nobody else ever made. Even if they were *noble* savages, which they are not, they would not be Steinbeck's heroes because they are incapable of the kind of moral involvement that can come about only through *conscious* recognition of the struggle between good and evil. George, not Lennie, confronts the impossibility of Lennie's rabbit-hutch-for-two dream; George must bear the pain of living, after he has killed Lennie to keep him safe from the world. As for Thomas, of course rituals seem like a trap to him since he is not, and has no reason to become, involved in the search for an unknown god. Joseph must seek the source of the stream in his glade in order to comprehend his place in the universal scheme of things; even Burton must leave to find his peace in an evangelist community. But Thomas need not search because he is himself one of the free spirits of the natural

[19]   *Ibid.*, p. 36.
[20]   *Ibid.*, p. 274.

world. In *Sea of Cortez* (quoted above, p. 23), Steinbeck wrote that
the feeling, the "mystical outcrying" we call religious, is man's
attempt to perceive his relation "to the whole thing, ... to all
reality, known and unknowable". Thomas, as a symbol of the
primitive, need not cry out because he has never strayed from
fundamental Nature; in sharp contrast with other men he instinctively *knows* his place in the universe.

Benjamin, the youngest of the brothers, may be distinguished
from Thomas as a lap dog is from a wolf; the edges of his instincts
have been dulled by pampering. A drunkard and a liar, he imposes
upon the kindness of those who, out of pity, build his house, feed
him and mother him. Women are always a little surprised to find
themselves seduced after he has used to his own ends their pity for
his weaknesses. His family does not mourn when, early in the
novel, caught in bed with Juanito's wife, Benjamin is killed by
Juanito's knife. In Benjamin, Steinbeck depicts one of the ways in
which man may be corrupted by civilization — through failure to
maintain pride in himself either as an animal or as a rational man.
Thomas is a symbol of physical man's struggle to preserve himself;
Joseph represents the best efforts of rational and spiritual man;
Burton and Benjamin, on the other hand, are tainted by diseases of
civilization, the one by strait-laced and arrogant puritanism and
the other by self-indulgent carnality.

Rama and Elizabeth, the wives of Thomas and Joseph, are alike
(though Elizabeth is younger and less experienced) as wise arche-
typal mothers and wives. Their religion is inextricable from their
femaleness and from their function as perpetuators of the race.
"'A whole plane of knowledge opens when a woman is carrying a
child. Rama told me'", Elizabeth says. And Joseph tells her that
although the child is precious, what is more so is the bearing of it;
"'that is a tie to the earth. ... It is proof that we belong here, ... the
only proof that we are not strangers.'"[21] And although their tie *is*
to the earth, they recognize Joseph as "'a symbol of the earth's
soul'", and they worship him as such. In Joseph's marriage to
Elizabeth, Steinbeck has created a parallel to the earlier union of
Joseph with the earth; in each case Joseph is dedicating himself to

[21]   *Ibid.*, p. 169.

the perpetuation of life. Ingeniously, Steinbeck includes Rama in his scheme just at the point when it would seem that the earth is dying and Joseph's mission is a failure. In quick succession, the tree dies, the drought kills off the cattle and the crops, and Elizabeth's life is suddenly ended when she breaks her neck in a fall. Joseph, at this time of need, goes to the pool in the glade to be reminded that the desolation is only one cycle coming to a close, that the earth does not die, and that his death (as all deaths) marks a new beginning. Rama is like the glade. With Elizabeth dead, there is still Rama, the great earth-mother who lives on, fulfiled by man and fulfiling man. In another symbolic copulation, when Joseph is desolate on the night of Elizabeth's death, Rama comes to him:

"It was a hunger in me, but a need to you. The long, deep river of sorrow is diverted and sucked into me, and the sorrow which is only a warm wan pleasure is drawn out in a moment."[22]

There is a striking parallel between the phenomenon that Rama here describes and that which takes place when Joseph cuts his wrists and lets his blood flow into the land. The hungry earth sucks up his blood and is nourished by it at the same time that Joseph's body grows light and is relieved of its sorrows and its life. Joseph literally returns to the earth, as he had done symbolically with Rama. And the final indication of Rama's symbolic role comes when she takes the son of Joseph and Elizabeth to raise as her own.

Steinbeck's three thematic courses have even in this early novel begun to intertwine and to form a pattern. The novel is of course concerned primarily with the religious directions given to a variety of men by their inner voices, and, as Edmund Wilson put it, Steinbeck "is dealing quite frankly with the destructive and reproductive forces as the central principles of all nature".[23] But concurrent with these concerns, Steinbeck, we find, has made Joseph into a special kind of hero — a hero, in fact, quite like the biologist-observer who was to become his standard, beginning with *In Dubious Battle*. Joseph, the reader may remember, even as his own

[22] *Ibid.*, p. 245.
[23] Edmund Wilson, *The Boys in the Back Room* (San Francisco, 1941), p. 49.

paganism-pantheism grows into a personal religious obsession to sacrifice himself for the continuance of mankind, is the only character in the novel who is fully conscious of what he is doing and who allows that each man must do as his nature bids him. What is sin for Burton, Joseph had said, is not sin for him. And when Joseph, as a kind of last resort to any available magic, goes to Father Angelo to ask him to pray for rain, Father Angelo tells him that he can only pray for Joseph's soul: Joseph is reminded again that other men's rituals will not do for him. Earlier, as Joseph watched an old hermit perform an animal sacrifice to the dying sun, he thought:

"What has this man found? ... Out of his experience he has picked out the thing that makes him happy." He saw the old man's joyful eyes, saw how in the moment of death he became straight and dignified and large. "This man has discovered a secret."[24]

Now this liberalism of Joseph's is the same kind of wide vision that is typical of Steinbeck's later heroes. When Burton asks Joseph to give up his pagan rituals, Joseph answers: "'I won't give up my thing to your thing. I won't swear to anything that limits me, that cuts down my activity.'"[25] And after Elizabeth dies, Rama tells Joseph that even though he loved Elizabeth he "didn't know her as a person. You never have known a person. You aren't aware of persons, Joseph, only of people. You can't see units, Joseph, only the whole.'"[26] As if to bear out Rama's words Joseph, at his death, symbolically merges with the whole: "'I should have known. ... I am the land ... and I am the rain. The grass will grow out of me in a little while.'"[27]

A concomitant of the Steinbeck hero is his isolation from humanity (the group animal) so that he may observe it whole. From this position, the hero invariably views life in non-teleological terms, thereby satisfying the third aspect of Steinbeck's thematic pattern and incidentally indicating to the reader Steinbeck's own thinking and esthetic methodology. Joseph is such a stranger —

---

[24] Steinbeck, *To A God Unknown*, p. 265.
[25] *Ibid.*, p. 205.
[26] *Ibid.*, p. 243.
[27] *Ibid.*, p. 322.

feared, respected and even worshipped, but above all, as Rama tells Elizabeth, never to be known. Rama continues:

"I do not know whether there are men born outside humanity, or whether some men are so human as to make others seem unreal. Perhaps a godling lives on earth now and then. ... I tell you this man is not a man, unless he is all men."[28]

And in the scene at the fiesta, Steinbeck describes the frenzied dancers as they join hands and seem like one great animal:

The dancers lost identity. Faces grew rapt, shoulders fell slightly forward, each person became a part of the dancing body, and the soul of the body was the rhythm.[29]

But Joseph stands conspicuously apart; "he felt tied to the dancing body, but he did not join it." Thomas, as a shy animal retreats from thunder, seeks the quiet of the barn; Burton, we have seen, cowers while he damns the pagans. Joseph, however, watches the dancers and exults because it brings them "'closer to the earth for a moment'" and, simply, because it makes them happy. He knows that these things are not to be feared, nor despised, but to be understood (nonteleologically) for what they *are*, what they might mean in themselves; they are, Joseph says, "'only indications how the world fares'".[30]

The rituals of men involved in searching for the identity of their souls are neither good nor bad, neither effectual nor ineffectual; they are only ways of giving to men some sense of their part in a whole scheme, a greater reality. Any of the characters in *To A God Unknown* might have answered as the old hermit did when asked why he performed his special ritual: "'I gave up reasons. I do this because it makes me glad. I do it because I like to. ... In the moment [that I sacrifice to the sun] I am the sun. Do you see?'"[31]

---

[28] *Ibid.*, p. 121.
[29] *Ibid.*, p. 160.
[30] *Ibid.*, p. 167.
[31] *Ibid.*, p. 266.

IV

IN DUBIOUS BATTLE:
NON-TELEOLOGY AND THE PSYCHOLOGY OF THE GROUP

In a subsequent chapter I shall discuss in some detail Steinbeck's several ventures into the comic spirit. It should be said now, however, that *Tortilla Flat*, his next novel after *To A God Unknown*, and his first attempt at full-length comedy, in no way interrupted the development of his basic themes. *Tortilla Flat* represents a "departure" only in the sense that its technique is social satire and its characters the mock-heroic *paisanos* of Monterey. Steinbeck's concern in the novel is still with the curious ritualism of men (only this time the rituals are a burlesque of social customs), with the tendency of men to form into groups in order to better their chances for survival (Danny and his friends work wonderfully well together in "finding" chickens and wine that belong to nobody in particular), and with the phenomenon of leadership (when Danny dies, the group disintegrates).

In its concern with the predatory ways of a commercialized society, even though those ways are seen through a mask of folly, *Tortilla Flat* even serves as a link with *In Dubious Battle*. For beneath its mask *Tortilla Flat* is certainly sympathetic to the underdogs, the cast-offs of that society, and in its emphasis upon social folly and injustice it gives us the first important clue to Steinbeck's growing recognition of the iniquities of the nineteen-thirties. With *In Dubious Battle* this concern came to rest on the dispossessed masses — the "working stiffs" of the great depression — where it was to remain through *Of Mice and Men* and *The Grapes of Wrath*. It is important to recognize, however, that *In Dubious Battle* is no mere proletarian tract, that it works on two levels, the social and the psychological.

Still, perhaps due to the passionate involvement of so many
critics and writers in the social upheavals of the nineteen-thirties,
In Dubious Battle was pegged as reform propaganda, and the mis-
designation has unfortunately survived despite a few critical
revaluations. Edwin Berry Burgum, for example, while he acclaims
the novel as "more lifelike and satisfying than. ... the dreary lot of
so-called proletarian novels of the thirties", arrives at a strictly
sociological conclusion:

(No documentary film in which the sophisticated) observer swallows the
document because the photography is so good, could be more successful
to win support for the striking ... workers in the great fruit-growing fac-
tories of the California plains.[1]

Burgum appreciates the novel's documentation of the strikers'
plight, but he does not see that Steinbeck's deeper interest in the
strikers is psychological and ecological. Carlos Baker, one of the
few critics who returned to the novel to study it when its social issue
had ceased to be quite so pressing, noted that Steinbeck's "larger
intentions" were with "what happens to men's minds when they
function, not as responsible, self-governing individuals, but as
members of a group. What happens to separate identities when
they merge into corporate identities?"[2] For the biologist, these are
problems of bionomics, or ecology. For Steinbeck, philosopher and
artist, as well as biologist, the problems also become psychological
and esthetic.

With the group of nine hundred strikers as the "control", *In
Dubious Battle* provides an esthetic testing ground for Steinbeck's
group-man theory and for its related aspects of the leader and of
the hero-biologist who observes with scientific detachment. The
novel is largely the story of a professional Communist organizer,
Mac, and his protege Jim, "who seek to function as the directive,
disciplinary force, the brain, for nine hundred striking men, an
extremely complex super-organism in which all those lesser individ-
ualities are merged".[3] As I have implied, the reader's sympathies

---

[1] Edwin Berry Burgum, "The Sensibility of John Steinbeck", *Science and
Society*, X (Spring, 1946), p. 137.
[2] Carlos Baker, "*In Dubious Battle* Revalued", *N.Y. Times Book Review*, July
25, 1943, p. 4.
[3] *Ibid.*

are aroused for the migrant fruit-pickers and their families who are oppressed by the owners, by the self-styled vigilantes, and by the police. When the workers do organize and strike for living wages, these opposing forces, together with the townspeople, who are incited by a reactionary press, themselves organize to drive away the "threat". But even while our sympathies are thus directed, Steinbeck leaves no room to suppose that Mac and the Communist Party provide an answer to the worker's plight. Mac, despite an occasional show of honest sentiment for the victims of capitalist exploitation, is a vicious exponent of Machiavellian opportunism. He knows from the beginning that the strike is doomed to failure, yet he is willing to sacrifice any and all who might be "used" to further the ends of the Party — to organize, to agitate, and to convert. It is Mac's job, using any means available to him, to gain the confidence of the workers, to make them believe that they democratically control themselves, to bring them to the edge of violence without ever letting them go over the edge, and finally, to leave them with a developed class consciousness and the belief that from their unity will come ultimate victory in a kind of social and economic millenium. Mac goes about his work with deliberate ruthlessness.

When Mac first enters the camp of disgruntled workers, depressed and dangerously suspicious of outsiders, he pretends experience in child delivery in order to gain an "in" with the men: "'That was a lucky break. We simply had to take it. 'Course it was nice to help the girl, but hell, even if it killed her — we've got to use anything.'"[4] He also uses the incident to begin his organization of the strike. When Jim, after the delivery, asks why it was necessary to burn all the clothes contributed by the men, even though much of it was not required, Mac answers:

"Look, Jim. Don't you see? Every man who gave part of his clothes felt that the work was his own. They all felt responsible for that baby. It's theirs, because something from them went to it. To give back the cloth would cut them out. There's no better way to make men part of a movement than to have them give something to it. I bet they all feel fine right now."[5]

4 John Steinbeck, *In Dubious Battle* (New York, 1936), p. 60.
5 *Ibid.,* p. 61.

To this same end of providing the men with the illusion of participation and control, but recognizing that the workers are wary of
Communists, Mac manipulates London, a respected but inarticulate
front man, into the position of "chairman". Seizing the moment
when the men are incensed because an old man has fallen from a
faulty ladder, Mac pushes forward with his organization of the
strike. He instructs London in "democratic" voting procedure:

"You give 'em a list of guys, about ten, and tell 'em to vote for those guys
as a committee to figure things out. ... If you want 'em to vote for something, you say 'do you want to do it?' and if you want to vote down
somethin', just say, 'you don't want to do this, do you?' and they'll vote
no. Make 'em vote on everythin', *everythin'*, see? They're all ready for
it."[6]

As the "brain" of the group now transformed from nine hundred
individual "cells" into one "big animal", Mac senses its despair
when the strike seems to be losing momentum. He knows just how
to revive the animal: fill its belly and show it blood. Party sym-
pathizers, contacted by agents in touch with Mac, supply the food;
vigilantes supply the blood by killing a punch-drunk old Party
organizer, Joy. Mac uses Joy's bloody body, first to reunify and
incite the strikers and later to gain public sympathy with a funeral
procession through town. Whenever the strikers' spirits begin to
wane, Mac resorts to a similar show of blood to enrage the "animal".
And at the novel's end, Mac even uses Jim's body, mangled by a
shotgun blast, to agitate the workers. Ironically, Jim had often
asked when Mac would get around to "using" him, and now,
despite the genuine friendship that had developed between the
two, Mac is as methodical as ever in displaying the faceless body.
Depositing the body on a platform, Mac "dragged Jim across the
boards and leaned him against the corner post, and steadied him
when he slipped sideways. ... London handed the lantern up, and
Mac set it carefully on the floor, beside the body, so that its light
fell on the head. He stood up and faced the crowd. ... 'Comrades!
He didn't want nothing for himself ...'"[7]

All of Mac's ruthless activities seem justifiable to him because he

[6]   *Ibid.*, p. 102.
[7]   *Ibid.*, p. 343.

has come to see that a group has a life of its own, different from its individual parts: "'It *is* a big animal. It's different from the men in it. And it's stronger than all the men put together. It doesn't want the same things men want."[8] But Mac likes to assume that his knowledge of the animal is nearly complete and that he can therefore direct it, at will, towards desired ends. He can rationalize his sacrifice of individuals, for example, on grounds that Steinbeck later investigated in *Sea of Cortez*: "It will be found that certain units are assigned special functions to perform; that weaker or slower units may even take their places as placating food for the predators for the sake of the security of the [whole] animal."[9] Unfortunately for Mac's idealistic ends, his knowledge and therefore his control of the animal is incomplete. Once the animal is created, "the best-laid strategical plans are often circumvented by bionomic unknowns". Mac's control "is no more absolute than the control of any reasonable mind over any potentially wayward body".[10] At times when the enraged animal seems about to turn on him, even Mac, its "master", concedes, "'it's swell when we can use it, but we don't know enough. When it gets started it might do anything.'"[11]

Mac's antagonist in the story is Doc Burton, at once a sort of chorus commenting upon the action, and a voice for Steinbeck. He combines in his character the iconoclastic, truth-seeking quality that was peculiar to Coeur de Gris in *Cup of Gold*, together with a sacrificial humanitarianism not unlike Joseph's in *To A God Unknown*; but in both of these qualities he is more fully developed than were either Coeur de Gris or Joseph. In Doc Burton, Steinbeck for the first time creates a hero who is in fact a man of science and who is thereby given a certain license to elaborate Steinbeck's scientific-philosophic theories of the group-animal and nonteleological thinking.

Because of Doc's insistence that he remain detached from partisan causes in order to "*see*" as much as he can of "the whole thing",

---

[8] *Ibid.*, p. 317.
[9] John Steinbeck, *Sea of Cortez* (New York, 1941), pp. 240-241.
[10] Baker, p. 16.
[11] Steinbeck, *In Dubious Battle*, p. 317.

his attitude towards the strikers and their leaders is necessarily ambivalent. "'I don't believe in the cause'", he tells Mac, "'but I believe in men'".[12] Because he has no illusions about the success of the strikers' cause, Doc cannot sanction Mac's brutality. Similarly ambivalent, because group-man must believe in the cause in order to survive, is the strikers' attitude toward Doc. As Mac puts it, "'If he wasn't a doctor, we couldn't have 'im around. We need his skill, but his brain just gets us into trouble. ... We've a job to do ... We've got no time to mess around with high-falutin ideas.'"[13] All the men, including Mac, nevertheless develop a special fondness for Doc Burton as they see him working selflessly for their welfare. And when he disappears, probably a victim of the vigilantes, he is sorely missed, not only because his work insured the camp decent sanitary conditions, but because his altruism has a saintliness about it that penetrates their hard-boiled idealism and makes them sense that their violent espousal of a cause is perhaps much less efficacious than Doc's undiscriminating tendance to any who need help. When Doc answers Mac's question about why Doc sticks with the men even though he has no faith in the cause, we are given a valuable insight into Doc's non-teleological approach to life, as well as into his altruism:

"I guess I just believe they're men, and not animals. Maybe if I went into a kennel and the dogs were hungry and sick and dirty, and maybe if I could help those dogs, I would. Wouldn't be their fault they were that way. You couldn't say, 'Those dogs are that way because they haven't any ambition. They don't save their bones. Dogs always are that way.' No, you'd try to clean them up and feed them. I guess that's the way it is with me. I have some skill in helping men, and when I see some who need help, I just do it. I don't think about it much. If a painter saw a piece of canvas, and he had colors, well, he'd want to paint on it. He wouldn't figure why he wanted to."[14]

This kind of action, based upon perceptual rather than conceptual motivation, is one of the results of nonteleological thinking and represents the essential difference between Doc and Mac. Steinbeck, as I noted above in Chapter I, wrote that "non-teleolog-

12   *Ibid.*, p. 194.
13   *Ibid.*, p. 147.
14   Steinbeck, *Sea of Cortez*, p. 135.

ical thinking concerns itself primarily not with what should be, or could be, or might be, but rather with what actually 'is' — attempting at most to answer the already sufficiently difficult questions *what* or *how*, instead of *why*".[15] Mac, the "practical" man, believes that he can posit what *should be* by first determining *why* a given situation exists. For example, Mac assumes that the economic straits of the proletariat are *caused* by the exploitation inherent in the profit system. *Therefore*, he concludes, if we do away with the profit system and replace it with communism (what "should be"), the evil will disappear. Mac justifies his cruelties with just such a proposition. Steinbeck was to detail the dangers of Mac's approach in *Sea of Cortez*:

In their sometimes intolerant refusal to face facts as they are, teleological notions may substitute a fierce but ineffectual attempt to change conditions which are assumed to be undesirable, in place of the understanding-acceptance which would pave the way for a more sensible attempt at any change which might still be indicated.[16]

Doc believes that such teleological thinking is futile because it presumes that causes and effects can be precisely evaluated so as to arrive at fixed conclusions. Knowing that matter is in perpetual flux and that at any given moment an effect may be seen simply as another cause in the endless search for *final* causes or effects, Doc counters Mac's belief that careful planning will result in the envisioned Utopia:

"There've been communes before, and there will be again. But you people have an idea that if you can *establish* the thing, the job'll be done. Nothing stops, Mac. If you were able to put an idea into effect tomorrow, it would start changing right away. Establish a commune, and the same gradual flux will continue."[17]

Doc prefers to accept what "is" and to understand as much of it as he can. " 'I don't want to put on the blinders of "good" and "bad", and limit my vision. If I used the term "good" on a thing I'd lose

[15]   Steinbeck, *Sea of Cortez*, p. 135.
[16]   *Ibid.*
[17]   Steinbeck, *In Dubious Battle*, p. 143.

my license to inspect it, because there might be bad in it'",[18] he tells Mac.

Doc's rejection of causality as a valid approach to positive action, and his refusal to involve himself in any social or philosophical movement that might limit his vision, appear on the surface to represent extreme passivity and isolation from the community of man. As Mac put it, "'If you see too darn much, you don't get anything done.'" But Steinbeck's conclusions are exactly the opposite. We have already seen how Doc, *accepting* conditions without wasting time trying to determine what caused them, can take "sensible" action on altruistic grounds. Steinbeck, speaking through Doc, argues that in reality it is the "practical" men of Mac's ilk, those who rely on causal (teleological) thinking, who get nowhere. In fact, these "practical" men (group men and their leaders) are so befogged by the illusion of total victory that they are apt to do more harm than good by justifying whatever means they choose to use towards their dubious ends. They do not see, as Doc does, that evil can lead only to more evil.

Along these same lines, Doc tries to explain to Mac how two major misconceptions about the nature of group-man (both of them indicative of the flaws in teleological thinking) doom the movement to failure. The first of these misconceptions is that a group fervently believes in its cause; the truth is, as Doc understands it, that the group is only reacting in the way that an animal reacts to glandular stimulation:

"When group-man wants to move, he makes a standard. 'God wills that we recapture the Holy Land'; or he says, 'We fight to make the world safe for democracy'; or he says, 'We will wipe out social injustice with communism.' But the group doesn't care about the Holy Land, or Democracy, or Communism. Maybe the group simply wants to move, to fight, and uses these words simply to reassure the brains of individual men."[19]

Mac, believing himself an expert on group psychology, does not understand the group's complex biological nature; he is ignorant of the "bionomic mysteries which result when one has joined nearly a

---

[18]   *Ibid.*
[19]   *Ibid.*, p. 145.

thousand men into a crowd".[20] Doc comments on this separate
physical life and how Mac's denial of it leaves only the illusion of
control:

"It might be worth while to know more about group-man, to know his
nature, his ends, his desires. They're not the same as ours. The pleasure
we get in scratching an itch causes death to a great number of cells.
Maybe group-man gets pleasure when individual men are wiped out in a
war.

. . . .
You practical men always lead practical men with stomachs. And something always gets out of hand. Your men get out of hand, they don't
follow the rules of common sense, and you practical men either deny that
is so, or refuse to think about it. And when someone wonders what it is
that makes a man with a stomach something more than your rule allows,
why you howl, 'Dreamer, mystic, meta-physician.' ... In all history there
are no men who have come to such wild-eyed confusion and bewilderment as practical men leading men with stomachs. ... You start your
work not knowing your medium. And your ignorance trips you up every
time."[21]

The second illusion under which practical men labor is that leaders
are solely responsible for group activity. "'How do you account for
people like me, directing things, moving things?'" Mac asks.
"'That puts your group-man out.'" Doc answers:

"You might be an effect as well as a cause, Mac. You might be an
expression of group-man, a cell endowed with a special function, like an
eye cell, drawing your force from group-man, and at the same time
directing him, like an eye. Your eye both takes orders from and gives
orders to your brain."[22]

Steinbeck later detailed this concept in *Sea of Cortez*:

The teleological notion would be that those in the forefront are leaders
in a given movement and actually direct and consciously lead the masses
in the sense that an army corporal orders "Forward march" and the
squad marches ahead. One speaks in such a way of church leaders, of
political leaders, and of leaders in scientific thought. ...
    Non-teleological notion: that the people we call leaders are simply
those who, at the given moment, are moving in the direction behind

[20] Baker, p. 4.
[21] Steinbeck, *In Dubious Battle*, pp. 146-147.
[22] *Ibid.*, p. 145.

which will be found the greatest weight, and which represents a future mass movement.[23]

One more parallel must be drawn between Steinbeck and his hero, Doc Burton: Steinbeck's esthetic method, his attitude towards his material, is composed of precisely that detached objectivity and scientific thoroughness that characterizes Doc. This approach is used (by both author and character) to give order and meaning to the activities of men who otherwise appear to be in violent and irrational flux. But despite the studied detachment of the technique, it will be found at its center to be motivated by Steinbeck's deep concern for the individual and for humanity. Peter Lisca provides an accurate account of the novel's prose strategy:

> The prose of *In Dubious Battle* is harsh, factual, catalogue-like in its complete objectivity. It does not soften the violence, but neither does it exploit it. ... Whether the action described is one of violence or tenderness, whether the scene is a sordid boardinghouse room or a beautiful apple orchard, the prose style is the same. It is a monotone which does not attempt either to soothe or jar the reader's sensibilities.[24]

It can easily be seen that this prose style is consistent, on an esthetic level, with the non-teleological philosophy voiced by Steinbeck and practiced by Doc Burton. The prose, so to speak, is also concerned with "seeing" the whole picture, and its tone does not tend to either sentimentalize or ennoble what it sees. And this is the point: the novel postulates no "answer"; it does not ask its readers to choose sides, for the outcome of the battle it depicts is indeed dubious. But it does allow the reader to see, in much the same way as Doc sees, beyond the illusions of those (like Mac and the strikers) who are deceived by their very involvement in the battle. And, again like Doc, the reader is led to a greater sympathy for the human predicament by virtue of his newly-acquired wide vision. The non-teleological approach, Steinbeck wrote in *Sea of Cortez*, involves more than a way of thinking; it involves a "*modus operandi* ..' a method of handling data of any sort. ... The method extends beyond thinking even to living itself." And, rather than

[23] Steinbeck, *Sea of Cortez*, p. 138.
[24] Peter Lisca, *The Wide World of John Steinbeck* (New Brunswick, N.J., 1958), pp. 116-117.

being hard-hearted or cruel, even though appearing coldly detached and analytical, "non-teleological methods more than any other seem capable of great tenderness, of an all embracingness which is rare otherwise".[25]

[25] Steinbeck, *Sea of Cortez*, pp. 146-147.

V

A FEW WORDS ABOUT "SOMETHING THAT HAPPENED"

Because the subject of *In Dubious Battle* was mass man, the preceding chapter was primarily concerned with Steinbeck's concept of group ecology; I discussed Steinbeck's interest in individuals only as far as they were either a part of the group (Mac the leader), merging with the group (Jim the novice), or observing the group (Doc Burton). But if Steinbeck found the group worthy of study because it was "more than the sum of its parts", he also knew that the individuals who composed the group must also be studied — if only because each is more than the sum of his cells, because each is a vital human being. So the question arises, because a group *is* men: What is it in the nature of men, considered as individuals, that motivates them to struggle towards ideals which are invariably lost in a shuffle of circumstances? The striking group of *In Dubious Battle* gets its energy, after all, from the hundreds of migrant workers — wanderers upon the earth — who have been dispossessed by natural and economic forces. What yearnings, what illusions must they share, must perhaps all men share, to make them turn their energy towards ends which are, at best, dubious?

Steinbeck's handling of these questions in *Of Mice and Men*, and his shift in focus from groups to individuals, will be better understood if I first examine certain thematic similarities between that novel and *In Dubious Battle*.

In Dubious Battle did not entirely bypass the individual's illusion. Implied by the action of men coming together to search for a world in which they would no longer be "migrants", is a great religious dream of utopian peace and prosperity. The strikers, we have seen, move on faith, resenting "high-falutin ideas" that might weaken their resolution. Even when Doc Burton gives a name to Jim's passionate faith in the illusion, Jim is resentful:

"You've got something in your eyes, Jim, something religious. I've seen it in you boys before."
   Jim flared, "Well, it isn't religious. I've got no use for religion."
   "No, I guess you haven't. Don't let me bother you, Jim. Don't let me confuse you with terms. You're living the good life, whatever you want to call it."
   "I'm happy", said Jim. "And happy for the first time. I'm full-up."
   "I know. Don't let it die. It's the vision of heaven."

The sense of fulfillment Jim feels when he is working with other men for a cause is later described by Doc as "pure religious ecstasy".[1]

In *Of Mice and Men* this theme is carried over and developed. Steinbeck focuses, instead of on the group, on two individuals, migrant workers who might well have been among the strikers of *In Dubious Battle* but who are now removed from the body of the group and examined as its microcosms. The strikers clung together to protect themselves from doubting the success of their utopian vision. Similarly, George and Lennie need one another to keep alive their dream of finding "a little piece of land" where they might cease their wandering and live in simple, domestic peace.

Steinbeck's technique in *Of Mice and Men* is still disciplined by his non-teleological methods of observing "phenomena". He is concerned not with the *why* but with the *what* and *how* of the individual's illusions. The title that Steinbeck originally intended for the novel, "Something That Happened", is a typically unsentimental comment upon the tragic reversal of fortunes experienced by George and Lennie. And the lines from Burns' poem, which provided the title finally used, even more explicitly illustrate the illusory condition of man's highest hopes:

But, Mousie, thou art no thy lane,
In proving foresight may be vain:
The best laid schemes o' mice an' men
   Gang aft agley
An' lea'e us nought but grief an' pain
   For promis'd joy.

[1] John Steinbeck, *In Dubious Battle* (New York, 1936), pp. 200, 254.

George and Lennie, like the strikers and like the mouse, are frustrated in their plans by the nature of things, by "something that happened". Since we can never track down the *cause* of life's ironies, both Steinbeck and Burns are saying, we had best accept them for what they *are* — conditions of human existence.

The theme of this novel, however, is not only its non-teleological observation that man is the victim of amoral Nature. This is something we know, if not from the title, then certainly after a very few pages of reading when we see how the well-intentioned Lennie cannot avoid destroying with his great idiot clumsiness all the simple things he loves most. Mindless Lennie is not responsible for what he does, but society nevertheless cannot tolerate him. Hence, when the old ranch hand, Candy, delivers his decrepit and foul-smelling dog into the hands of his bunk-mates, to let them kill the dog mercifully, we know that Lennie will have to die for his socially obnoxious act of violence. Lennie's unintentional destructiveness will therefore block his dream of tending the rabbits on the farm where he and George would "live on the fat o' the land". The failure of the dream, in fact, is implied by Lennie's tendency to crush the small animals he loves to feel and which he intends only to stroke.

But *Of Mice and Men* may also be read as a social protest and as an allegory. Peter Lisca efficiently summarizes the first as "Steinbeck the reformer crying out against the exploitation of migrant workers", and the second as an

interpretation limited only by the ingenuity of the audience. It could be, as Carlos Baker suggests, "an allegory of Mind and Body."[2] Using the same kind of dichotomy, the story could also be about the dumb, clumsy, but strong mass of humanity and its shrewd manipulators. ... (or) that of the unconscious and the conscious, the id and the ego, or any other forces or qualities that have the same structural relationship to each other that do Lennie and George.[3]

These symbolic interpretations may suggest to the reader that the

---

[2]   See Carlos Baker, "Steinbeck of California", *Delphian Quarterly*, XXIII (April, 1940), p. 42.
[3]   Peter Lisca, *The Wide World of John Steinbeck* (New Brunswick, N.J., 1958), p. 139.

relationship between George and Lennie closely resembles that which existed between Mac and the strikers in *In Dubious Battle*. The ranch hands often ask the intelligent George why he bothers to burden himself with Lennie. What they do not see is that George "uses" Lennie to sustain his own dream of the farm, that if he did not believe that Lennie needed him for protection his illusion would dissipate under the pressures of the workaday world. Without the "earth longings"[4] of the primitive, asocial Lennie, George would fall prey to the literally hopeless life pattern of his peers. His faithfulness to Lennie belies his words: "'God a'mighty, If I was alone I could live so easy. ... I could take my fifty bucks and go into town and get whatever I want. Why, I could stay in a cat house all night. I could eat anyplace I want ... , get a gallon of whiskey, or set in a pool room ...!' " But when Lennie pathetically offers to leave him alone, George responds quickly: "'No — look! I was jus' foolin', Lennie. 'Cause I want you to stay with me.'"[5] George (seen as mind) is just as certainly welded to Lennie (seen as body) as Mac (the "brain" of the group animal) is to the body of strikers. Both George and Mac want to believe that they control the great primordial forces with which their own fates are bound; for only if they do control can they make progress towards their dream worlds. Mac attempts to use the strikers in ways that will aid the cause of communism; George puts Lennie to work to earn money needed to buy a farm. As we have seen, the carefully laid plans of Mac and George get nowhere because the forces they would manipulate are as unpredictable and uncontrollable as Nature itself.

There is another way in which *Of Mice and Men* may be likened to *In Dubious Battle*, and that is in its inclusion of Slim, a character whose qualities we recognize as similar to those of Doc Burton. There is one major difference: in the evolution of his hero type, Steinbeck has made Slim less of a talker than Doc and more of a doer, more of a man of the people; less of an abstract "voice" and

---

[4]   John Steinbeck in a letter to his agents, September, 1936. Cited by Lewis Gannett in "John Steinbeck's Way of Writing", Introduction to *The Portable Steinbeck* (New York, 1946), p. xvii.
[5]   John Steinbeck, *Of Mice and Men* (New York, 1937), pp. 23-24, 27.

more of an individual in his own right. Still, like Doc, he is gentle, understanding, and quietly wise in his acceptance of the way things are. We see him in this passage as he first appears to the reader:

Like the others he wore blue jeans and a short denim jacket. When he had finished combing his hair he moved into the room, and he moved with a majesty only achieved by royalty and master craftsmen. He was a jerkline skinner, the prince of the ranch, capable of driving ten, sixteen, even twenty mules with a single line to the leaders. ... There was a gravity in his manner and a quiet so profound that all talk stopped when he spoke. His authority was so great that his word was taken on any subject, be it politics or love. ... His hatchet face was ageless. He might have been thirty-five or fifty. His ear heard more than was said to him, and his slow speech had overtones not of thought, but of understanding beyond thought.[6]

Slim does not participate in George's dream, perhaps because he has no need for it in his position of honor on the ranch. But this is only to say that Slim's "understanding beyond thought" includes an acceptance of what *is*, which removes him from the futile struggle to remake the world as it *should be*. Thus detached, Slim is the only one who is capable of seeing George's tragic loss when George is forced to kill Lennie to save him from the mob. George kills a part of himself, the part that was his dream. Slim comforts George with a gentle reminder that it is better to kill the dream yourself ("'a guy got to sometimes'"[7]) than to deliver it into the hands of society, who would tear it apart in order to preserve itself.

I have been trying to illustrate that *Of Mice and Men* bears a strong thematic and structural relationship to *In Dubious Battle*. Both stories involve the hopeless pursuit of an illusion — the same illusion. As social protest, both decry the maltreatment of migrant laborers. The allegorical structure of each is based upon Steinbeck's group-man theory and its conjunctive aspect of leadership (the several possible interpretations of the allegory stemming from the conflict that arises when an intellective force attempts to impose its will upon its mindless physical counterpart.) Finally, both novels are fictive enactments of Steinbeck's non-teleological philosophy; no blame or cause is ascribed to the patterns of action, and a

---

[6]   *Ibid.*, pp. 61-62.
[7]   *Ibid.*, p. 185.

dispassionate narrator in each case describes the action simply as "something that happened". To give credence to this philosophy, Steinbeck includes in each novel a character whose non-teleological view of life illustrates dramatically what is otherwise an abstraction.

What, however, differentiates *Of Mice and Men* from *In Dubious Battle?* What makes it a work of greater emotional impact even though its thematic and philosophic concerns are almost identical with those of its predecessor? The answers seem to lie, as I implied in the first page of this chapter, in the earlier novel's reliance on protagonists of an organically *impersonal* nature. Steinbeck depended, for allegorical effectiveness, upon characters and groups of characters that were nearly flat representations of ideological forces. For example, much more important than "roundness" in the character of Doc Burton is his personification of intellectual independence. It is the tensions that arise between these ideational forces when they are placed in a setting of violent social flux, rather than "human" elements of conflict, that invite the reader's excitement. In contrast, *Of Mice and Men* focuses upon two individuals who, while they serve allegorical purposes, retain their individuality. George and Lennie are unusual characters, but they are believable. And because they are believable their tragedy also seems real and gains the reader's sympathy. Burton Rascoe, discussing Steinbeck's handling of character, writes:

[Lennie is] a believable contemporary figure — a man who would be described on any police docket ... as a sexual pervert or degenerate and in almost any psychiatrist's case history as, probably, a man afflicted with gigantism, with an abnormally low I.Q., unusual thyroid deficiency, excessive pituitary secretion with resulting imbalance, a tactile fetish, psychic and/or physical impotence, and with improperly functioning adrenals which caused him in moments of fear to act destructively without intention — and Steinbeck chose to, and did, make this mostrosity a sympathetic figure, one whom you, if you had heart in you, would regard with all the despair but also with all the affection with which the giant Lennie is regarded by ... the more astute and intelligent George.

And about George, Rascoe continues:

George has toward Lennie the tenderness and the protective instinct which some of even the most hard-bitten and most hardboiled have toward the helpless, the maimed, the dependent. A lonely, itinerant bindle-stiff, a migratory ranch hand, barley bucker, mule skinner, fruit picker, and general handy man, without a home or family, George has encountered and embraced a ... humanitarian responsibility. It is to take care of, protect, save from hurt, the dim-witted, loyal, and devoted Lennie.[8]

Lennie, however, is not merely a moron of fantastic strength, and George is not merely his bindlestiff protector. Their search for a safe place away from a world they never made is, after all, a ritual act as old as man himself. The dialogue between George and Lennie, recurring in almost identical language whenever either of them feels despondent, is like the chant of a priest and the response of his congregation. It is the ritual of earth-bound man listening to and being reassured by his hopeful inner voice:

George's voice became deeper. He repeated his words rhythmically as though he had said them many times before. "Guys like us, that work on ranches, are the loneliest guys in the world. They got no family. They don't belong no place. ... They ain't got nothing to look ahead to."
Lennie was delighted. "That's it — that's it. Now tell how it is with us."
George went on. "With us it ain't like that. We got a future. We got somebody to talk to that gives a damn about us. ... If them other guys gets in jail they can rot for all anybody gives a damn. But not us."
Lennie broke in. "*But not us! An' why? Because ... because I got you to look after me, and you got me to look after you, and that's why.*" He laughed delightedly. "Go on now, George!"
"You got it by heart. You can do it yourself."
"No, you. I forget some 'a the things. Tell about how it's gonna be."
"O.K. Someday — we're gonna get the jack together and we're gonna have a little house and a couple of acres an' a cow and some pigs and ..."
"*An' live off the fatta the lan.*"[9]

It is a curious thing that audiences to the play, which Steinbeck adapted from the novel with only minor changes, invariably laughed at the antics of dimwitted Lennie — but that the laughter was short-lived; before the end of the first act compassion had replaced their "light, superficially cynical mood". The audience

[8] Burton Rascoe, "John Steinbeck", *The English Journal*, XXVII (March, 1938), 208-209.
[9] Steinbeck, pp. 28-29.

changed as, despite themselves, "pity and wonder [took] possession of them".[10] The experience is, it seems to me, no different for the reader of the novel; he begins with the reader's typical attitude of detachment from the fictional events before him, but before long he is in sympathy with the tragically shattered illusions of George and Lennie, perhaps because he sees in them something of his own illusions and his own tragedy.

[10] Rascoe, p. 208.

VI

THE GRAPES OF WRATH

Let there be no doubt that *The Grapes of Wrath* is a novel of protest. Steinbeck saw firsthand the dumping of oranges and potatoes and the burying of slaughtered pigs while hungry people looked on, forbidden by law to touch. He saw people uprooted from their land by incomprehensible natural and economic forces, saw them turned into homeless migrants, tormented and shunned like lepers by self-styled vigilantes who feared that their own precarious economic and social security might be infected by contact. Perhaps worst of all, Steinbeck saw people as their dignity slipped away from them.

We may say of this novel that it is the work of a craftsman skilled in storytelling; we may probe the craftsmanship to discover its symbolic complexities and say that this novel is really about a spiritual pilgrimage; we may find in the novel's concern with massive group movement and with group leadership a further development of Steinbeck's basic themes; and, by logical extension of these themes, we may see them as they reflect several traditional American ideas — Emerson's self-reliance, Whitman's love of the democratic masses, Jefferson's agrarianism, and William James' pragmatism.[1] Still, when we have taken this novel and laid it out piece by piece for critical examination, when we have seen its structure, its symbols, its philosophies, and its themes, we will know then that these bared facts are not the reasons why this is one of those rare novels impossible to forget. When we are through with our examination and we put the pieces back together and look

[1] See Frederick Carpenter, "The Philosophical Joads", *College English* II (January, 1941).

again at the whole, we will rediscover what we knew after first reading *The Grapes of Wrath*: that its powerful and lasting effects result from its vivid depiction of social and cosmic conditions which seek to rob men of their humanity, and that its effects result also from the fact that we identify ourselves with Steinbeck's characters as they struggle to resist those conditions.

We should not confuse Steinbeck's protest with what is ordinarily called "propaganda". Steinbeck is not concerned with the endless maze of causes for his Okies' being driven from their land and made destitute. You can take your choice of causes — soil erosion, the economic system, human greed, sinfulness — and find yourself no closer to the truth. Nor does Steinbeck map a way out of the labyrinth of human misery. You can put your faith in any of several palliatives — soil conservation, Communism, love, virtue — but none of these will effect a final cure. Steinbeck advocates no social philosophy. Nevertheless, because of what it tells of the nature of evil, his novel is social protest. Perhaps, as Joseph Warren Beach has said, "the best of social philosophies, so far as fiction is concerned, is that which comes spontaneously to the lips of people trying to figure out a way through life's labyrinth. The best sort of story from the point of view of sociology is one that by the very nature of its incidents sets you pondering the most fundamental human problems".[2] Steinbeck goes first to the "incidents", studies them, tries to see as much as he can of their inherent evil. For example, of starvation in the midst of plenty, he writes:

There is a crime here that goes beyond denunciation. There is a sorrow here that weeping cannot symbolize. There is a failure here that topples all our success. The fertile earth, the straight tree rows, the sturdy trunks, and the ripe fruit. And children dying of pellagra. ... [3]

And then Steinbeck goes to the victims of the crime to see what is happening to them, to see if they will lapse into passive discouragement or if they will shake off their early bewilderment, grow angry, and fight for survival. He finds that "in the eyes of the hungry there

[2] Joseph Warren Beach, *American Fiction: 1920-1940* (New York, 1941), p. 328.
[3] John Steinbeck, *The Grapes of Wrath* (New York, 1939), p. 477.

is a growing wrath. In the souls of the people the grapes of wrath are filling and growing heavy, growing heavy for the vintage."[4]

In the depiction of this determination of the common people to survive, one may detect an important new development in Steinbeck's group-man theme. Until now Steinbeck's groups have had no will of their own, have had no control over their direction. The strikers of *In Dubious Battle* had an alien social philosophy thrust upon them and, as we have seen, the attempt to control them failed because the leaders were out of touch with the group, because they refused to see what the group really wanted. The "animal" did not want Communism; it wanted to feed its empty stomach. And in *Of Mice and Men*, as the title implies, George and Lennie are at the mercy of chance, their pipe dream doomed because George does not know how to channel the vagaries of Lennie. In *The Grapes of Wrath*, however, leaders emerge from the people; they have no separate wills of their own but represent the general will of the mass. If a leader is killed, this does not matter because the group's will to survive is not dependent upon any one of its members; leaders are easily replaced. In the same way, rather than disintegrating when one of its goals is lost, the group adapts itself to the new condition and grows stronger as its hardships increase. Two years after *The Grapes of Wrath* Steinbeck wrote:

Where there is little danger, there seems to be little stimulation. Perhaps the pattern of struggle is so deeply imprinted in the genes of all life conceived in this benevolently hostile planet that the removal of obstacles automatically atrophies a survival drive. With warm water and abundant food, the animals may retire into a sterile sluggish happiness. This has certainly seemed true in man. Force and cleverness and versatility have surely been the children of obstacles.[5]

These ideas are dramatized in *The Grapes of Wrath* in the persistent struggle of the common people, represented by the Joads, to endure in the face of overwhelming obstacles. And their determination to endure does not rest entirely upon a blind instinct; these are people increasingly *aware* of their position, people who consciously *will*

[4] *Ibid.*
[5] John Steinbeck and Edward F. Ricketts, *Sea of Cortez* (New York, 1941), p. 227.

their survival, who know that their survival depends upon purposiveness and unity. When the Joads have to decide whether to take Jim Casy with them to California, even though it means an extra mouth to feed, Ma answers for the family:

"It ain't kin we? It's will we?" she said firmly. "As far as 'kin', we can't do nothin', not go to California or nothin'; but as far as 'will', why, we'll do what we will."[6]

And earlier, after the first numbing shock of losing their land had passed,

the faces of the ... men lost their bemused perplexity and became hard and angry and resistant. Then the women knew that they were safe and that there was no break. ... The men sat in the doorways of their houses; their hands were busy with sticks and little rocks. The men sat still — thinking — figuring.[7]

Several elements of structure in *The Grapes of Wrath* are closely tied to this theme of the group's willful action. The first element is simply that the book is a "road" novel describing the migrants as they prepare for their departure, journey southwest to California in search of greener pastures, and arrive in California only to discover that in order to survive they must keep moving to wherever work is available. As this broad framework implies, the migration is purposeful; it is necessitated by circumstances, but as the migrants think and talk about what is happening to them it becomes a dynamic means to a better life. "'People moving'", Casy says. "'We know why, an' we know how. Movin' 'cause they got to. That's why folks always move. Movin' 'cause they want somepin better'n what they got. An' that's the on'y way they'll ever git it. Wantin' it an' needin' it, they'll go out an' git it.'"[8]

A second structural element that supports the idea of willful movement in the novel, is Steinbeck's frequent use of interchapters to integrate the particular story of the Joad family's migration with the vast background of social upheaval of the nineteen thirties. Chapter 12, for example, presents a panoramic view of the great

6 Steinbeck, *The Grapes of Wrath*, p. 139.
7 *Ibid.*, pp. 6-7.
8 *Ibid.*, p. 173.

migratory activity along Highway 66, describing in motion-picture detail the flight of families in over-loaded jalopies — the privations, the injustices at the hands of profiteering merchants, the pleasure taken from occasional kindness. Then Chapter 13 shifts easily back to the Joad's actual journey. Chapter 29 describes the coming of winter to California — the heavy rains, the flooded land, and the resulting layoffs of the migrant farm laborers. And Chapter 30, the final chapter, returns us to the Joads, who are now trapped by the flood in an abandoned box-car where Rose of Sharon's baby is born dead. Even in this desparate situation the Joads will not stay put; they *move* to an abandoned barn in order to survive. Here, in the novel's last symbolic action, Rose of Sharon gives to a starving man the milk intended for her baby.

Peter Lisca points out that "this integration of the interchapters into a total structure goes far beyond a merely complementary juxtaposition. There is in addition an intricate interweaving of specific details. ... Every chapter is locked into the book's narrative portion by ... specific cross-reference, which amplifies the Joad's typical actions to the dimensions of a communal experience."[9] By his choice of details within this linking structure, Steinbeck manages to foster in the reader a sense of onward-flowing progress. The famous description of a turtle crossing the highway (Chapter 3), for example, symbolizes the heroic persistence of the migrants to keep moving against overwhelming odds. The turtle's journey, like that of the migrants', is accompanied by life and death incidents: the turtle snaps in its head, simultaneously killing a red ant and picking up a sprig of wild oats which later falls out and is planted in the ground across the road. And like the migrants the turtle meets with kind and vicious acts: the driver of one car swerves to avoid hitting the turtle, but another driver goes out of his way to try to run over it. Despite the obstacles, the turtle continues to plod along on its southwesterly journey, the same direction taken by the migrants.

In Chapter 4 the symbolic value of the previous episode is enhanced when Tom Joad picks up the turtle to take it home for

[9] Peter Lisca, *The Wide World of John Steinbeck* (New Brunswick, N.J., 1958), pp. 157-158.

the children. When he learns that his family has left the land, Tom releases the turtle and it again takes up its southwest direction. Significantly, Tom is described as plodding along, "dragging his cloud of dust behind him", his bare feet scraping in the fine dust. Then Tom meets Jim Casy who is pictured with "a long head, bony, tight of skin, and set on a neck as stringy and muscular as a celery stalk. His eyeballs were heavy and protruding; the lids stretched to cover them, and the lids were raw and red. ... The nose, beaked and hard, stretched the skin so tightly that the bridge showed white".[10] The turtle's symbolic identification with the migrants is made complete when Casy comments on its unyielding efforts to keep moving: "'Nobody can't keep a turtle though. They work at it and work at it, and at last one day they get out and away they go — off somewheres.'"[11] And in Chapter 14, in terms similar to those in which he described the turtle's progress, Steinbeck speaks of man's ability to endure great changes:

This you may say of man — when theories change and crash, when schools, philosophies, when narrow dark alleys of thought, national, religious, economic, grow and disintegrate, man reaches, stumbles forward, painfully, mistakenly sometimes. Having stepped forward, he may slip back, but only half a step, never the full step back.[12]

Several episodes in *The Grapes of Wrath* are concerned with what happens when individuals or groups *fail* to take willful action against adversities. These episodes constitute a third structural element in support of the novel's theme of purposeful, directional movement. The first such episode centers on Muley Graves who, because he chooses to remain behind on the barren land and because he refuses to adjust to new conditions, comes to represent a *type* of man doomed to extinction. Even his name suggests his symbolic role: Muley (obstinate), and Graves (the resting place of the dead). Tom and Preacher Casy come upon Muley hiding out on the deserted land he had once farmed, his family and friends

---

[10] Steinbeck, *The Grapes of Wrath*, pp. 26-27.
[11] *Ibid.*, p. 28.
[12] *Ibid.*, pp. 204-205. (None of the novel's sixteen interchapters equals this one in its didacticism. Although it is spirited and inspiring prose, its subjectivity is inconsistent with the otherwise objective approach of the rest of the novel.)

already started on their westward migration. Muley cannot let go of the past; he has never revived from the shock of tractors overrunning his land:

"An' I got wanderin' aroun'. Jus' walkin' aroun'. Never went far. Slep' where I was. ... I'd tell myself, 'I'm lookin' after things so when all the folks come back it'll be all right.' But I knowed that wan't true. There ain't nothin' to look after. The folks ain't never comin' back. I'm jus' wanderin' aroun' like a damn ol' graveyard ghos'."[13]

In sharp contrast to Muley, Casy (whose role as a guiding spirit of the migration I shall detail later) is hopeful of finding a new life for himself by joining the Joads on their journey: "'Yeah, I'm goin' with you. ... An' where folks are on the road, I'm gonna be with them.'" But when Tom asks Muley to join the family, Muley answers: "'No. I don't go no place, an' I don't leave no place.'"[14] Truly, he goes no place; Muley will perish because he will not adopt the underdog's only survival techniques — migration to more productive land and aggressive action against those who dominate the land.[15] In a final, symbolic act of the episode, Muley offers to share his pathetic retreat in the earth with Tom and Casy. Tom answers, "'I ain't gonna sleep in no cave.'" But Muley "pulled at the covering brush and crawled into his cave. 'I like it in here', he called. 'I feel like nobody can come at me.'"[16] Hiding, Muley is most vulnerable to the onrush of circumstances.

A second episode, when the Joads are at the Weedpatch camp, pursues the idea that the group's survival chances are small if it allows itself to be lulled by false security. The episode is also important as a refutation of the popular belief that *The Grapes of Wrath* was intended as a socialist tract outlining the way to Utopia. In *Sea of Cortez*, after praising the "stolid, sluggish endurance" of a lone shark that had been caught but still "would not release life", Steinbeck suggests that complete standardization, as that which occurs in some schools of fish, results in a mass mediocrity which

[13] *Ibid.*, p. 69.
[14] *Ibid.*, p. 77.
[15] Steinbeck, *Sea of Cortez*, pp. 94-96.
[16] Steinbeck, *The Grapes of Wrath*, p. 82.

eliminates the survival instinct typical of the individualistic shark. He then applies the thought to man:

In a thoroughly collectivized state, mediocre efficiency might be very great, but only through the complete elimination of the swift, the clever, and the intelligent, as well as the incompetent. Truly collective man might in fact abandon his versatility.[17]

Something of this sort happens to the Joads during their month's stay in the government-run migrant camp at Weedpatch. (Here, after the hardships and indignities suffered at "Hoovervilles" throughout California, they find a communal haven.) At Weedpatch there are no cops (the people maintain a police force of their own); there is hot water and there are inside toilets; there is a community fund to tide over the destitute; and there are Saturday night dances. Nobody would deny that these things are good; as Ma Joad puts it, "'Why, I feel like people again.'"[18] But discontent creeps into this communist haven, and Ma is the first to recognize its signs. (The men brood because they can find no work; they grow listless and hide their shame at having to take charity; they disappear after breakfast to avoid facing the fact that they will have to abandon the material comforts of collective civilization. But Ma revives their anger and their spirit: "'You ain't got the right to get discouraged. This here fambly's goin' under. ... We got to git goin', an' goin' quick. I ain't a-settin' here no longer, no matter how nice.'"[19] And then, speaking to Tom about her reasons for angering the men, Ma says:

"Take a man, he can get worried an' worried, an' it eats out his liver, an' purty soon he'll jus' lay down and die with his heart ct out. But if you can take an' make 'im mad, why, he'll be awright. Pa, he didn' say nothin', but he's mad now. He'll show me now. He's awright."[20]

By moving on when the illusion of security threatens to make the family soft, the group retains its vitality and increases its chances for survival in a hostile world. Ma's words again remind us that the nature of Steinbeck's group in *The Grapes of Wrath* has changed

[17] Steinbeck, *Sea of Cortez*, pp. 213-214.
[18] Steinbeck, *The Grapes of Wrath*, p. 420.
[19] *Ibid.*, pp. 479-480.
[20] *Ibid.*, p. 481.

from the dumb, blind, misled "animal" of *In Dubious Battle* into a thinking, self-led collection of individuals who have *willingly* banded together to fight in a common cause. It is this common cause, in fact, which puts group-man's individuality to the test. "I believe", wrote Steinbeck for *The Saturday Review*, "that man is a double thing — a group animal and at the same time an individual. And it occurs to me that he cannot successfully be the second until he has fulfilled the first."[21]

It might indeed be said, after examining the structure of *The Grapes of Wrath*, that Steinbeck views man as a triple thing — an individual, a part of a specific group, and a part of macrocosmic humanity. The device of interchapters is used in part to gather the Joad family (composed of unit-individuals) into the mass of migrating humanity. Chapter 17, describing the migrants as they move, family by family, into a campsite, is particularly illustrative of this merging process:

In the evening a strange thing happened: the twenty families became one family, the children were the children of all. ... Every night a world created, complete with furniture — friends made and enemies established; a world complete with braggarts and with cowards, with quiet men, with humble men, with kindly men. Every night relationships that make a world, established.[22]

Steinbeck detailed the esthetic advantages of this microcosm to macrocosm method when in 1941 he wrote the story for *The Forgotten Village*, a pictorial book made from a documentary film about a Mexican village. In the Preface, Steinbeck wrote:

A great many documentary films have used the generalized method, that is, the showing of a condition or an event as it affects a group of people. The audience can then have a personalized reaction from imagining one member of that group. I have felt that this is the more difficult observation from the audience's viewpoint. It means very little to know that a million Chinese are starving unless you know one Chinese who is starving. In *The Forgotten Village* we reversed the usual process. Our story centered on one family in one small village. We wished our audience to know this family very well, and incidentally to like it, as we

[21] John Steinbeck, "Some Thoughts on Juvenile Delinquency", *The Saturday Review* XXXVIII (May 28, 1955), p. 22.
[22] Steinbeck, *The Grapes of Wrath*, pp. 264-265.

did. Then, from association with this little personalized group, the larger conclusion concerning the racial group could be drawn with something like participation. Birth and death, joy and sorrow, are constants, experiences common to the whole species.[23]

"The point of the whole novel", Frederic Carpenter wrote of *The Grapes of Wrath*, "is that action is an absolute essential of human life."[24] Well, whether or not it is *the* point, it certainly is a central point and a pervasive motif. I have indicated how in this novel Steinbeck included in his group-man theme the idea that the group, if it is to survive, must be more than just so many cells joined to form a mindless, mechanistic "animal"; it must be, instead, a body united by a common will to survive, but nevertheless composed of men who keep their separate identities. Those groups which are motivated by fear and which have become tools — whether they are the big farm owners who are the tools of the social system, or vigilantes who are in turn the tools of the owners — are destined to die out because "they have become de-humanized, have lost the vitality and initiative and adaptability of good biological specimens of the human species". They become "so sunk in the social organism as to lose ... biological individuality".[25]

Along with these changes in Steinbeck's conception of group-man, comes a corresponding change in the nature of his leaders and heroes. We have already seen how, prior to *The Grapes of Wrath*, Steinbeck created clean lines of distinction between the group, the leader, and the hero. The strikers of *In Dubious Battle*, for example, were out to satisfy their basic hunger for security; Mac, the leader, was interested in the strikers only as they served his ideological ends; and Doc Burton, the biologist-hero, found it necessary to detach himself from group and leader before he could serve humanity in his own way. In *The Grapes of Wrath* Steinbeck brings about a curious and productive merging of these three forces.

First of all (as I noted above, p. 68), since the migrant group is

[23] John Steinbeck, "Preface", *The Forgotten Village* (New York, 1941).
[24] Carpenter, p. 323.
[25] Frederick Bracher, "Steinbeck and The Biological View of Man", *Steinbeck and His Critics*, ed. W. W. Tedlock and C. V. Wicker (Albuquerque, 1957), p. 196.

created with a conscious will, leaders emerge from within the group
to represent that will; they are no longer intruders, as Mac was.
When we recall Steinbeck's belief that a man cannot be a successful
individual until he has first been a group-man, it becomes easier to
understand how the group continually nurtures its potential
leaders. If a leader is lost, there are others to take his place. The
men of the migrant families, traditionally the leaders, often falter
from the great weight of their burden; but women like Ma Joad,
trained by years of suffering hardships silently, are prepared to
hold the family-group together until the men are once again ready
to assume responsibility. At one point, when Tom seems ready to
kill a deputy sheriff who had been vulgarly insulting, Ma restrains
him, knowing that uncontrolled violence would give the police
the opportunity they looked for to destroy the feared unity of the
migrants. Her faith is characteristic of Steinbeck's new leader:
"'Easy', she said. 'You got to have patience. Why, Tom — us
people will go on livin' when all them people is gone. ... They
ain't gonna wipe us out. Why, we're the people — we go on.'"[26]

As a second step in the process of merging group, leader, and
hero, Steinbeck invests his leader with characteristics which had
heretofore been reserved exclusively for his biologist-hero. Besides
being group-born (and therefore one with the aims of the group),
honest, and genuinely sympathetic to human suffering — all of
which qualities have been lacking in Steinbeck's leaders — the
leader is now endowed with the ability to view life with non-
teleological calmness, with "the love and understanding of instant
acceptance" which leads, not to stifling passivity, but to wise and
considered activity. In the following description of Ma Joad one
may recognize the attitudes of Steinbeck's biologist-hero:

Her full face was not soft; it was controlled, kindly. Her hazel eyes
seemed to have experienced all possible tragedy and to have mounted
pain and suffering like steps into a high calm and a superhuman understanding. She seemed to know, to accept, to welcome her position, the
citadel of the family, the strong place that could not be taken. ... And
from her great and humble position in the family she had taken dignity
and a clean calm beauty. From her position as healer, her hands had

<hr />

[26] Steinbeck, *The Grapes of Wrath*, p. 383.

grown sure and cool and quiet; from her position as arbiter she had become as remote and faultless in judgment as a goddess.[27]

There is a third step to this merging process, a step which necessitates a close look at the role played by Jim Casy, first in his direct relationship with the group and then in his far more important symbolic role within the novel's Biblical structure. Steinbeck had given his leader nearly heroic dimensions when he provided Ma Joad with the altruism and insight described above; but he did not displace his typical hero. By creating a set of circumstances which join Jim Casy, at first an outsider, to the body of the group, Steinbeck manages to complete the union of group, leader, and hero, even as he keeps alive the hero's separate identity by giving him extra dimension — spiritual dimension beyond even the qualities we have seen in the earlier "typical" heroes. We are once again reminded of Steinbeck's proclamation that before a man can realize himself as an individual he must first become a group-man. At the beginning of the book, Casy is already as fully developed as any of the previous Steinbeck heroes. He has disengaged himself from an active role in society by forswearing his evangelistic preaching in favor of a life of speculation. (As Casy puts it, "Got a lot of sinful idears — but they seem kinda sensible.") After his sojourn in the wilderness ("like Jesus went into the wilderness to think His way out of a mess of troubles"), Casy's ideas have not entirely set, but he has arrived at the stage required of all Steinbeck's heroes: he has rejected absolutes in order to see the larger picture. He has, in effect, become a non-teleological thinker:

"There ain't no sin and there ain't no virtue. There's just stuff people do. It's all part of the same thing. And some of the things folks do is nice, and some ain't nice, but that's as far as any man got a right to say."[28]

Now if Casy had remained static at this point, he would have been equal to the task of being a Steinbeck hero; he would have been the novel's disinterested observer, unselfishly helping the migrants — as long as his right to be detached was not questioned. But Casy, Steinbeck's *new* hero, takes an unprecedented step for his type: he joins the group, immerses himself in the vital activity of the

[27] *Ibid.*, p. 100.
[28] *Ibid.*, p. 32.

migrants, decides to travel with them wherever they go. His acceptance into the Joad family is given ritual significance. Tom speaks for the family:

"We think long as you're goin' with us, you ought to be over with us, helpin' to figger things out."
    Casy got to his feet. He knew the government of families, and he knew he had been taken into the family. Indeed his position was eminent, for Uncle John moved sideways, leaving space between Pa and himself for the preacher. Casy squatted down like the others, facing Grampa enthroned on the running board.[29]

Once again, if Casy were to remain permanently as a member of the Joad family, his role in the novel would be limited to something like that of Ma Joad's as a combination leader-hero. In one sense Casy and Ma Joad meet halfway in order to complete the merging of group, leader, and hero: Ma emerges to leadership from *within* the group, becoming the ideal leader because she brings with her the pragmatism born of her years of hard experience, and because she finds a great vision of human dignity; Casy descends into the group, moving "from the purely speculative to the pragmatic".[30] He already has the vision of dignity; now he is searching for the means to implement it. He finds those means in the world of action as it is represented in the experiences he shares with the Joads, and his discovery provides him with a new gospel to preach — the gospel of an Oversoul and of the unity of all men. Symbolically, Casy is separated from the Joads at a moment when his mission appears clear to him. He offers himself as a sacrifice by accepting the blame when Tom knocks out a deputy who had badgered the migrants and shot a migrant woman. When Casy leaves the Joad family (the microcosm), he becomes a spokesman for the family of man (the macrocosm).

    It is a logical next step to examine Casy's role as a Christ figure within the novel's overall Biblical structure. After what I have said of the importance to the novel of group movement, group action, and group unity, it might be expected that that Biblical structure is based upon the great migration of the Israelites from Egypt as it is

[29]   *Ibid.*, p. 140.
[30]   Lisca, p. 174.

described in Exodus. Several critics have noted the parallel; Peter Lisca describes it thus:

The novel's three sections correspond to the oppression in Egypt, the exodus, and the sojourn in the land of Canaan. ... This parallel is not worked out in detail, but the grand design is there: the plagues (erosion), the Egyptian (banks), the exodus (journey), and the hostile tribes of Canaan (California).[31]

Further, the novel's title is taken directly from "The Battle Hymn of the Republic" ("He is trampling out the vintage where the grapes of wrath are stored"), which, of course, refers to parts of the Bible for its inspiration and language. In Revelation (14:19), for example, "the angel thrust in his sickle into the earth, and gathered the vine of the earth, and cast it into the great winepress of the wrath of God". Perhaps more significant to the novel's theme of action born of anger, in Jeremiah (31:29) we find: "The fathers have eaten sour grapes, and their children's teeth are set on edge."

When Ma Joad vigorously and proudly asserts that "We are the people", she is reflecting the attitude that sustained the Israelites in their days of troubled flight. And it is noteworthy that when Grampa is buried the preacher reads a verse from Psalms (95:7): "For he is our God; and we are the people of his pasture." This "chosen people" motif is pervasive in the novel and suggests several possibilities: the migrants, like the people of Israel, are "chosen" to wander in search of a promised land, to suffer indignities as a test of their right to survive (the *Joad* family sounds curiously like the *Job* family), to receive a new code of law from which to build their new world ("Then leaders emerged, then laws were made, then codes came into being."[32]), and finally, chosen to bring forth a Christ who will preach a new faith. Jim Casy is that Christ.

There is, first of all, some "obvious" evidence in the novel of Steinbeck's intentions to create Jim Casy as a Christ symbol. Casy's initials are J.C.; like Jesus, Casy goes into the wilderness to meditate; like Jesus, Casy rejects his "eye for an eye" religion and preaches instead a gospel of love ("'I only love people'", Casy says. "'An' sometimes I love 'em fit to bust, an' I want 'em to make

[31] *Ibid.*, p. 169.
[32] Steinbeck, *The Grapes of Wrath*, p. 265.

happy.'")[33] Ma Joad makes us alert to Casy's special role when, early in the novel, after one of Casy's unusual graces, "she watched him as though he were suddenly a spirit, not human any more, a voice out of the ground",[34] And in the scene when he is killed, the parallel to Jesus is clear. Casy says, "'They figger I'm a leader 'cause I talk so much.'" Then, caught in the glare of flashlights, he is identified by the vigilantes as "'that shiny bastard'". His final words, before he is beaten to death, are "'You fellas don' know what you're doin.'"[35]

Martin Staples Shockley has done the most complete job to date of tracing Christian symbolism and Casy's role as a Christ figure through the novel.[36] Significantly, Mr. Shockley emphasizes that "Jim Casy's religion is innocent of Paulism, of Catholicism, of Puritanism".[37] Casy preaches a non-denominational and unorthodox religion that finds its roots in the peculiarly American intellectual tradition of blending mystical thought with pragmatic action. As we have seen, Casy's idealism becomes real for him only after he turns from the speculative life to the active life within the migrant movement. Frederic I. Carpenter contributes some important insights to Steinbeck's use of these traditional American ideas:

They [the ideas] continue, develop, integrate, and realize the thought of the great writers of American history. Here the mystical transcendentalism of Emerson reappears, and the earthy democracy of Whitman, and the pragmatic instrumentalism of William James and John Dewey. And these old philosophies grow and change in the book until they become new. They coalesce into an organic whole. And, finally, they find embodiment in character and action, so that they seem no longer ideas, but facts. ... Jim Casy translates American philosophy into words of one syllable, and the Joads translate it into action.[38]

I have said that Casy, when he leaves his old religion to go among the people to preach to them, is like Jesus; of course, he is also like

[33] *Ibid.*, p. 32.
[34] *Ibid.*, p. 111.
[35] *Ibid.*, pp. 526-527.
[36] See Martin Staples Shockley, "Christian Symbolism in *The Grapes of Wrath*", College English XVIII (November, 1956), 87-90.
[37] *Ibid.*, p. 88.
[38] Carpenter, p. 316.

Emerson who left his ministry to preach what he knew intuitively about the unity of mankind. Casy, who knows (as Emerson knew) that he "'can't hold no church'" with such unorthodox ideas, preaches not only fundamental Christian love, but an equivalent of the Emersonian oversoul as well: "'Why do we got to hand it on God or Jesus? Maybe ... it's all men and women we love; maybe that's the Holy Sperit — the human sperit — the whole shebang. Maybe all men got one big soul ever'bod's a part of. Now I sat there thinkin' it, an' all of a suddent — I knew it. I knew it so deep down that it was true, and I still know it.'"[39]

To better appreciate Casy's role as a transcendentalist, we need only think back to what I have said about Steinbeck's group-man theme as a pervasive element of structure in *The Grapes of Wrath.* The more obvious reason for Steinbeck's emphasis on family unity and on the unity of the migrants as a whole, is that only through united action could the underdogs better their social conditions. When Casy joins the group he learns that lesson; but he also perceives how the group's *physical* unity is an indication of the *spiritual* unity of all men. In the following passage Casy speaks of his revelation, and in it we may hear overtones, not only of Emersonian transcendentalism, but of Whitman's democracy and of the pantheism common to both of these American poets:

"There was the hills, an' there was me, an' we wasn't separate no more. We was one thing. An' that one thing was holy. ... I got thinkin' how we was holy when we was one thing, an' mankin' was holy when it was one thing. An' it on'y got unholy when one mis'able little fella got the bit in his teeth an' run off his own way, kickin' an' draggin' an' fightin'. Fella like that bust the holiness. But when they're all workin' together, not one fella for another fella, but one fella kind of harnessed to the whole shebang — that's right, that's holy."[40]

Casy's affirmation of democracy (as Whitman's) does not depend upon the destruction of the individualist. Rather, the individualist consciously and pragmatically dedicates himself to the survival of the group in order to assure his own spiritual survival. When Tom Joad, Casy's disciple and spiritual successor, leaves his family to

[39] Steinbeck, *The Grapes of Wrath,* pp. 32-33.
[40] *Ibid.,* p. 110.

join the larger social body of migrants, he has learned Casy's lesson
that each man's "little piece of a soul wasn't no good 'less it was
with the rest, an' was whole. ... I know now a fella ain't no good
alone." Tom will "live" because his life becomes a part of all life.
Ma says to him: " 'They might kill ya an' I wouldn't know.' "
And Tom answers:

"Then it don' matter. Then I'll be all aroun' in the dark. I'll be ever'-
where — wherever you look. Wherever they's a fight so hungry people
can eat, I'll be there. Wherever they's a cop beatin' up a guy, I'll be there.
If Casy knowed, why, I'll be in the way guys yell when they're mad an' —
I'll be in the way kids laugh when they're hungry an' they know supper's
ready. An' when our folks eat the stuff they raise an' live in the houses
they build — why, I'll be there. See? God, I'm talkin' like Casy. ...
Seems like I can see him sometimes."[41]

"Man", wrote Steinbeck, "unlike any other thing organic or inor-
ganic in the universe, grows beyond his work, walks up the stairs of
his concepts, emerges ahead of his accomplishments".[42] *The Grapes
of Wrath* is Steinbeck's affirmation that man's life has meaning
beyond material existence. And it is revealing of Steinbeck's
development as an artist and as a thinker that these conclusions,
implicit in *The Grapes of Wrath*, arise out of the same rational and
scientific approach to life with which I have identified him all along.
His method is non-teleological and phenomenological; he seems to
be saying that the events in the novel are things that happened, that
they are the patterns that he observed and found common to the
specie, man. But here one must stop and realize that *The Grapes of
Wrath* is no scientific treatise. Steinbeck converts his biological
approach into esthetic method. The physical phenomena he observes take on metaphorical meaning beyond their simple existence
as facts within a mathematically ordered universe. Man is man
because he has the ability to *perceive* his position in the macrocosm,
to perceive that he is "related to the whole thing". Man discovers
and reaffirms "that all things are one thing and that one thing is all
things".[43] And it is this discovery of the physical unity of all things
that provides him with his faith in a vast spiritual unity.

[41] *Ibid.*, p. 572.
[42] *Ibid.*, p. 204.
[43] Steinbeck, *Sea of Cortez*, p. 217.

VII

THE WAR AND A FEW YEARS AFTER

Immediately after the publication of *The Grapes of Wrath* came the inevitable charges of lewdness, inaccuracy, and blasphemy, levelled against it by 100 per cent Americans of politics, pulpit, and press, and by those various social and civic groups who take upon themselves the burden of defending the public morality and the national economy.[1] It was unfortunate that sensational controversies over the book as propaganda doomed any chance that it would, in its own day at least, be considered on its merits as a novel. But Steinbeck was far from dismayed. It had been one of his major purposes to shed light on a serious social injustice, and the controversial publicity raised the number of the book's readers into the millions.

But if wide public recognition of his novel pleased Steinbeck, attempts to lionize him made him shudder. He held sacrosanct his private life and his artistic integrity. It was this determination for self-preservation that hastened his departure with Ed Ricketts to the Gulf of California on the scientific expedition that led to the writing of *Sea of Cortez*. Publicity, however, was not the only incentive to withdrawal to the sea. Steinbeck was dismayed over the senseless killing that had already begun in Europe and that he was certain would soon infect the world: a war "which no one wants to fight, in which no one can see a gain — a zombie war of sleepwalkers which nevertheless goes on out of all control of intelligence".[2] He reasoned further that if we were to observe our own

[1] See Martin Staples Shockley, "The Reception of *The Grapes of Wrath* in Oklahoma", *American Literature*, XV (January, 1954), 351-361.
[2] John Steinbeck and Edward F. Ricketts, *Sea of Cortez* (New York, 1941), p. 88.

species as we observe, for example, hermit crabs or crayfish, we would have to conclude from the available evidence of our past and present that "our species is not likely to forego war without some psychic mutation which at present, at least, does not seem imminent. ... So far the murder trait of our species is as regular and observable as our various sexual habits."[3] The fact is not weakened, he added, by another "diagnostic trait" of our species — hope; the hope that our drive towards self-extinction may not always be.

Despite the assertion of one critic that *Sea of Cortez* is "the least social of Steinbeck's books ... in which he kills off all his remaining social compulsion and emerges into a perfect scientific vacuum",[4] Steinbeck is here reaffirming ideas which had been developing since his earliest work. And although he admits that the trip was in part a flight from publicity and war, it is clear from the anguished tone of his conclusions about man's murder instinct that the expedition was also intended to provide him with a clearer perspective of the indignities that the world was suffering in its blind pursuit of destruction. If his approach to life was still non-teleological and objective, it was not because he suddenly wished to detach himself from humanitarian obligations; it was, rather, a sign of his consistent belief that the way to effective action was to gain the widest possible vision of a given situation. He returned to the microcosmic tidepool so that he might better understand the nature of man's relation to the universe. *Sea of Cortez*, he wrote to his agents, "is a good clearing-out of a lot of ideas that have been working on me for a long time".[5] The book synthesized in "scientific" terms ideas that he had been dealing with for years in dramatic terms: non-teleology, the group animal, the survival instinct of animals and men, unconscious racial memories, the limitations of reason, and the unity of all things.

In *The Grapes of Wrath* Steinbeck had illustrated how groups could effectively insure their survival in a predatory society only if they sustained a conscious will to survive and only if they followed

---

[3] *Ibid.*, p. 17.
[4] Stanley Edgar Hyman, "Some Notes on John Steinbeck", *Antioch Review*, II (Summer, 1942), 190.
[5] Lewis Gannett, "Introduction", *The Portable Steinbeck* (New York, 1946), p. xxv.

leaders whose individuality provided them with a clear sight of the
purposes of their struggle. These twin necessities satisfied, man
could in fact inch forward in material and spiritual evolution. It
is no wonder then that Steinbeck reacted bitterly to the war, a war
"out of all control of intelligence". War, for Steinbeck, was futile.
He believed, as Doc Burton had expressed it in *In Dubious Battle*,
that "you can only build a violent thing with violence". Men in war
are not group men exercising their survival instinct, but are "herd
men" fed on the illusion that killing will end the killing, all the while
manifesting their drive towards self-extinction. Steinbeck recognized "the sad trait of self-destruction that is in our species", but
he denounced it. In what appears now to have been an almost
symbolic last act before the United States entered the war, Steinbeck
returned to Mexico immediately after his marine expedition to work
on the documentary, *The Forgotten Village*. The film was a poignant
illustration of man's potential for helping his fellow man to wage a
different kind of war — a war against ignorance, poverty, and
disease.

THE WAR EFFORT

If war is prime human folly, if the ends can never justify the means,
men nevertheless join it when it comes. Steinbeck, no different from
most who recognize its tragic waste, joined the war even though he
never wholly believed in it, and certainly he did not believe in its
slogans which urged men to fight for the glory of this or that. A
dozen years after it was over, Steinbeck was able to look back and
recall some of the reasons why he did not run from the conflict:
"Although all war is a symptom of man's failure as a thinking
animal, still there was ... some gallantry, some bravery, some kindliness."[6] His concern was again with *what* men did rather than with
why they did it.

Still, there is something pathetic about *Bombs Away*, Steinbeck's
first contribution to the war effort, a propaganda work for the Air
Force. It is pathetic because it compromises drastically the serious

[6] John Steinbeck, *Once There Was a War* (New York, 1958), p. xx.

and complex ideas he had employed in the esthetic patterns of his fiction. The book is a factual account of the training of a bomber crew — and it is a faithful account as far as that goes. But when Steinbeck attempts to force the application of some of his earlier themes upon the artificial situation of training for war, those themes are debased by sentimentality and rationalizations. A few examples from the text will illustrate this point.

In his Introduction Steinbeck tells his readers that the depression years had caused in the youth of the nation "a curious and muscling state of mind which was considered intellectual despair, but which was actually the product of mental and physical idleness".[7] This national softness represented the same kind of "weak survival quotient" by which Steinbeck had characterized species doomed for extinction. Even the migrants of *The Grapes of Wrath* were complacent to the point of dying with their dying land — until their security was threatened by the monster banks and they rose to the challenge. In *Bombs Away* Steinbeck tried the same formula, but somehow it did not work, perhaps because the cliches of the war propagandist (the pep-talk jargon and the generalizations about "our side") can never be more than highly partisan half-truths. "In attacking us", Steinbeck continued, Germany and Japan

destroyed their greatest ally, our sluggishness, our selfishness, and our disunity. The attack on us set in motion the most powerful species drive we know — that of survival. ... The goal has been set now and we have an aim and a direction, and a kind of fierce joy runs through the country. The President set an end in production that was almost beyond reason and that end is being reached. The General Staff designed an army like none in the world and that army is being assembled and trained.[8]

A year earlier Steinbeck would have shrugged off any suggestion that his concept of the survival instinct could be used to justify military regimentation and industrial mobilization for war.

Another of Steinbeck's themes gone awry in *Bombs Away* is that of the group as a unit. Again Steinbeck is accurate as he describes the separate training of each member of the bomber crew. And he is convincing when he explains that the crew is really a "team"

[7]   John Steinbeck, *Bombs Away* (New York, 1942), p. 13.
[8]   *Ibid.*, pp. 14-15.

which, if it is to function at all, "must function as a unit". But I must confess a certain embarrassment while reading about these things today — the sort of embarrassment one might feel while watching an old war movie on television and remembering how passionately involved he had once been in what now appears as a pack of melodramatic cliches. *Bombs Away*, like the old war movie, provides all the stereotypes. Al, the gunner, is a "tough little man from a small town in the Middle West" who (of course) once jerked sodas in the local candy store. Abner, the aerial engineer, had learned his skill from a correspondence school course and had run a garage until the war came. Joe, the pilot, is a big, South Carolina farm boy, clean cut and intelligent. One member of the ground crew comes, inevitably, from Brooklyn. This idealization of the martial spirit, under the guise of national group unity, is perhaps best exemplified in Steinbeck's description of how Bill, the bombardier cadet, comes to join the Air Force "team":

At first he had disliked the formations, but as he became precise in his step and carriage he grew to like them; the beat of the step, the numbers of men all acting in precise unison, became a satisfying thing to him. He discovered something he had not learned, which the directionless depression had not permitted him to learn — the simple truth that concerted action of a group of men produces a good feeling in all of them.[9]

Bombs Away no doubt served its purpose well. It was "intended to be read by the mothers and fathers of the prospective Air Force men, to the end that they will have some idea of the training their sons have undertaken".[10] But the mothers and fathers wanted more than a report on the technical features of their sons' training. They wanted the illusion sustained that all was right with the war and with their sons' participation in it. They wanted their war sugar-coated, and Steinbeck was willing to let them have it their way. It was not wrong that Steinbeck should have written a book for the Air Force; it is only unfortunate that in doing so he intruded so flagrantly upon his own ethical and esthetic standards.

Steinbeck's year of war reporting for the *New York Herald Tribune* was a much more fruitful venture. From England, North

[9]   *Ibid.*, p. 49.
[10]   *Ibid.*, p. 5.

Africa, and Italy, in 1943, his communiques centered on the "human interest" of the war. Hampered by the immediacy of his own involvement and by a discipline new to him, censorship, he nevertheless was vigorously honest in dealing with the events around him. It is significant, however, that fifteen years later, in the Introduction to a collected edition of his war stories, he felt compelled to discuss the kind of unreality that pervaded his writings of the war years:

Reading them over after all these years, I realize not only how much I have forgotten but that they are period pieces, the attitudes archaic, the impulses romantic, and, in the light of everything that has happened since, perhaps the whole body of work untrue and warped and one-sided.

The events set down here did happen. But on rereading this reportage, my memory becomes alive to the other things, which also did happen and were not reported. That they were not reported was partly a matter of orders, partly traditional, and largely because there was a huge and gassy thing called the War Effort. ...

For what they are worth, or for what they may recapture, here they are, period pieces, fairy tales, half-meaningless memories of a time and attitudes which have gone forever from the world, a sad and jocular recording of a little part of a war I saw and do not believe, unreal with trumped-up pageantry. ...[11]

Unlike *Bombs Away*, these articles do not gloss over the loss of individuality of men in war. Steinbeck's tone is, I feel, depressed and bitter as he describes the embarkation for England of thousands of American troops. The event itself, of weary, shuffling men being herded aboard ship by military police who have "handled this problem of traffic before", is inherently undignified. The men in their helmets, "which make them all look alike, make them look like long rows of mushrooms ... , have no identity, no personality. The men are units in an army ..., mushrooms in a bed of mushrooms."[12] And two days later, at sea, Steinbeck wrote:

Men cannot be treated as individuals on this troopship. They are simply units which take up six feet by three feet by two feet, horizontal or vertical. So much space must be allotted for the physical unit. They are engines which must be given fuel to keep them from stopping.

[11]   Steinbeck, *Once There Was a War*, pp. xi, xx.
[12]   John Steinbeck, "Dispatches from the European War Theater", *New York Herald Tribune*, June 20, 1943, p. 1.

Whether or not it was realized by Steinbeck's readers back home, descriptions of this kind were protests against a situation wherein men lost their identities and became herd men.

Even when Steinbeck is relating the humorous episodes of Private Big Train Mulligan, there are critical overtones of the bureaucratic machinery of war — red tape and red-faced staff officers. Big Train is a wartime Danny (the hero of *Tortilla Flat*); he is a precursor of "the boys" of *Cannery Row*. "Having decided (1) that he couldn't win the war single-handed, (2) that the war was going to last quite a long time, (3) that he wasn't going to get home on any given day, and (4) what the hell anyways, the Big Train settled down to enjoy what he couldn't resist."[13] Big Train's job is to chauffeur officers in a jeep. A confirmed goldbrick, he somehow manages to make the army work for him. When his officers dismiss him for dinner, he dines on roast beef and good wine while they eat soggy English vegetables and drink warm beer. He leaves his charges to lumpy mattresses in damp little inns while he seeks out some of the friends he had made here and there and is provided with a comfortable bed and clean white sheets.

Steinbeck likes Big Train. Not because he is good; he is not. But because he is curiously unhypocritical in refusing to call his pleasures by another name; because he survives by beating the army (and the civilized world) at its own game of self-interest; and because he symbolizes the struggle of the individual against regimentation and officialdom. What Steinbeck wrote two years later about Mack and the boys was also his attitude toward Big Train Mulligan:

Mack and the boys ... are the Virtues, the Graces, the Beauties of the hurried mangled craziness of Monterey and the cosmic Monterey where men in fear and hunger destroy their stomachs in the fight to secure certain food, where men hungering for love destroy everything lovable about them. ... In the world ruled by tigers with ulcers, rutted by strictured bulls, scavenged by blind jackals, Mack and the boys dine delicately with the tigers, fondle the frantic heifers, and wrap up the crumbs to feed the Sea Gulls of Cannery Row. What can it profit a man to gain the whole world and to come to his property with a gastric ulcer, a blown prostate, and bifocals? Mack and the boys avoid the trap, walk around

13   *Ibid.*, July 25, 1943, p. 1.

the poison, step over the noose while a generation of trapped, poisoned, and trussed-up men scream at them and call them no-goods, come-to-bad-ends, blots-on-the-town, thieves, rascals, bums.[14]

The reader may begin to see the several ways in which Steinbeck's war reports are more than mere journalism. In tone, characterization, and theme, these pieces bear the weight of comparison with Steinbeck's fiction; he undoubtedly recognized these qualities when he called the stories "fairy tales" and published them, as if they were a collection of his short stories, under the title, *Once There Was A War*. Structurally, too, this book is not unlike the plan of *The Pastures of Heaven*, *Cannery Row*, and *Tortilla Flat*, each of which, as Peter Lisca points out, is "loose and episodic", "similar in theme and setting", but held together by a thin thread of plot.[15] Steinbeck contributes further support for believing that his war stories may be read more as fiction than as journalism, when he tells of the detached point of view from which they were written:

All of us war correspondents developed our coy little tricks with copy. Reading these old pieces, I recognize one of mine. I never admitted having seen anything myself. In describing a scene I invariably put it in the mouth of someone else. ... Perhaps I felt that it would be more believable if told by someone else.[16]

Few writers equal Steinbeck as a storyteller, and perhaps one of the reasons that his reports from the war still make good reading is that almost all of them have the quality of parables. For example, the almost but not quite funny story of the tailgunner who loses his good luck medallion before his crew takes off on a raid, is meant to represent the mysterious part that superstition plays in man's life. The whole crew is made uneasy by the loss, and although no one even bothers to ask whether it was a religious medal or simply a good luck charm, all vigorously join in the search for the lost object. If they fail to find it, the crew will remain restless throughout their flight, and, if they run into bad luck, that will be blamed on the lost medallion. Steinbeck's emphasis on this kind of incident is

[14]   John Steinbeck, *Cannery Row* (New York, 1945), p. 9.
[15]   Peter Lisca, *The Wide World of John Steinbeck* (New Brunswick, N.J., 1958), p. 199.
[16]   Steinbeck, *Once There Was A War*, p. xvi.

typical of his concern with irrational behavior; he accepts the instinctive, the intuitive, and the ritualistic acts of man as being at least as important in life as the rational. The airmen's superstition in the episode of the lost medal may be linked with other "religious" incidents, throughout Steinbeck's fiction, which depict men foregoing rational means in favor of personal, mystical means of understanding their relationship to the universe. To recall just a few such instances: Joseph Wayne in *To a God Unknown* discovers his identity through his fetishistic devotion to a piece of land and to a tree; the Pirate in *Tortilla Flat*, rejected by the world of men, is nevertheless certain of his own salvation because he believes that his dogs have visions of Saint Francis and intercede in his behalf; and Jim Casy, by means of his transcendentalism, identifies himself with "all things" and all time.

The quest of men for identity and dignity, Steinbeck often seemed to be saying in his dispatches, is intensified by the pressures and tensions of war. Confronted with the unfamiliar and the uncontrollable, men fumble for personal symbols of permanence, often finding them in the trivia of everyday existence. One story, for example, tells of the incorrigibility of bombed-out Dover Englishmen, two of whom are, for a moment, more concerned over the damage to a rose bush than they are over the wrecked houses around them. The bush becomes a symbol for them. "Sometimes", says one of rose bushes, "when they've had a shock, they come out prettier than ever".[17] And in another story a Londoner, lying flat in a gutter during an air raid, finds a dead bird beside him, picks it up, and holds it for a long time. The man cannot tell why he did this thing, but Steinbeck explains: "It is as though the mind could not take in the terror and the noise of the bombs and the general horror and so fastened on something small and comprehensible and ordinary."[18] The very same symbols that these characters created to supply order to their disrupted lives, became Steinbeck's symbols for senseless killing and for the whole "crazy hysterical mess" of the war.

In March, 1944, four months after returning from Europe,

[17] Steinbeck, *Tribune*, July 6, 1943, p. 17.
[18] *Ibid.*, July 10, 1943, p. 7.

Steinbeck completed *Cannery Row*. As I have shown, after the documentary *Bombs Away* Steinbeck came to regard the term "war effort" as an invention of the propagandists designed to sustain the public's illusion of the war's rightness. It is doubtful, therefore, that in this frame of mind Steinbeck could have intended *Cannery Row* solely as light entertainment for the war weary — though such has been the contention of several critics. It is certainly a funny book, and Steinbeck himself has said that it was written at the request of soldiers, sick of war, who wanted something funny to read that wasn't about the war.[19] Nevertheless, Steinbeck did not sacrifice his serious ironic and satiric intentions to purposeless jesting or mildly humorous ribaldry. I see *Cannery Row* much in the same tradition as Erasmus' great ironic work, *The Praise of Folly*, and equally as much in the tradition of Apuleius.

Robert Graves, in the Introduction to his translation of *The Golden Ass*, speaks of a style employed by Apuleius which may easily apply to Steinbeck's method in *Cannery Row*: both have effectively employed the style of professional story-tellers delivering "street-corner entertainments". Both "found that the popular tale gave them a wider field for their descriptions of contemporary morals and manners, punctuated by philosophical asides, than any more respectable literary form".[20] It is probable, moreover, that *Cannery Row* will retain its popularity on the basis of its surface humor and bawdiness, the same basis on which rests the lasting popular interest in *The Golden Ass*. But this observation only reaffirms that Steinbeck's method is intentionally comic; it in no way impairs the fact that his comedy is, at its heart, serious.

Leonard Dean takes note of the common error of readers either to dismiss *The Praise of Folly* "as another straddling utterance by a man who ... never took a stand", or to misinterpret the irony as jesting "which has lost whatever serious point it may have had".[21] *Cannery Row* has suffered from the same kind of shallow reading. Steinbeck, however, like Erasmus, recognized that "irony may be

[19]   John Steinbeck, "My Short Novels", *Wings* (October, 1953), p. 8.
[20]   Robert Graves, Introduction to *The Golden Ass of Apuleius* (New York, 1951), pp. vii-viii.
[21]   Leonard Dean, Introduction to Erasmus, *The Praise of Folly* (New York, 1949), p. 2.

serious and that it may be the most direct and accurate mode of expression for complex ideas".[22] If Steinbeck seems mellow towards the degenerate characters of *Tortilla Flat*, it may be because, as Professor Dean writes of Erasmus, "he had a warm sympathy for confused and erring men"; but it will be equally true that "few human hypocrisies and pretensions escaped his censure".[23] Steinbeck himself, as Antonia Seixas reports, did not hesitate to support Malcom Cowley's suspicion that *Cannery Row* was a "'very poisoned cream puff'. If Cowley had read it again, said Steinbeck, he would have found how very poisoned it was."[24]

Those who recall Mack and the boys' frog hunt adventure, or their roaring "surprise" birthday party for Doc, will agree that the cream puff is delicious humor. The poison is the ironic fact that the reader finds himself where, by society's standards of correct behavior, he ought not to be — in sympathetic league with Steinbeck's failures and outcasts, the "blots-on-the-town, thieves, rascals, bums". Now what Steinbeck has done, by means of an artful double deception, is this: he has made his rascals so light-hearted and so free of conventional, civilized restraints that we envy them the freedom we have not got. And we like them. Not in spite of their rascality and thievery, but because we take pleasure in their successful forays against the restrictions of a society that we do not always like but that we almost always feel bound to by habit. Mack and the boys not only have the integrity needed to combat social regimentation, they have the independence needed to ignore the society almost as if it did not exist. The effect of all this is to make us wonder whether, having cast out the misfits and renegades, they are not indeed the better men, and whether, in fact, we have not cast them to where we wish we were — on the outside, quite free.

Steinbeck's rationale for this ironic juxtaposition may be seen in *Sea of Cortez* where he writes of an "ethical paradox" in the human situation:

[22]   *Ibid.*, p. 3.
[23]   *Ibid.*, p. 15.
[24]   Antonia Seixas, "John Steinbeck and the Non-Teleological Bus", *Steinbeck and His Critics*, ed. E. W. Tedlock and C. V. Wicker (Albuquerque, 1957), p. 276.

Of the good, we think always of wisdom, tolerance, kindliness, generosity, humility; and the qualities of cruelty, greed, self-interest, graspingness, and rapacity are universally considered undesirable. And yet in our structure of society, the so-called and considered good qualities are invariable concomitants of failure, while the bad ones are the cornerstones of success.[25]

Mack and the boys have those qualities requisite to "failure" in this scheme, and that is why Steinbeck called his heroes the "Virtues ... of the hurried mangled craziness of Monterey". They are kind and generous to the extreme of turning all their attentions and pooling all their assets to cure an ailing mongrel puppy. They are humble in the presence of Doc's superior intellect and fatherly concern for them, and, in fact, the party for Doc grows out of their honest desire to repay him for his goodness (and for having wrecked his laboratory when their first party for him "got out of hand".) They are tolerant in the way that only Steinbeck's non-teleological men can be: they do not have to forgive the faults of others (including the ambitiousness and covetousness of the world from which they are excluded) because they accept people as they are without trying to know why they act as they do. And they are wise because they refuse to undermine their own integrity by accepting society's hypocritical values. Of their wisdom, Doc says:

"All of our so-called successful men are sick men, with bad stomachs, and bad souls, but Mack and the boys are healthy and curiously clean. They can do what they want. They can satisfy their appetites without calling them something else. ... Mack has qualities of genius. They're all very clever if they want something. They just know the nature of things too well to be caught in that wanting."[26]

When Mack and the boys lie or steal they do so because they know that society does not tolerate altruism or honesty. For example, the owner of the property where the boys go to hunt their frogs is unmoved when they tell him that the frogs are needed for humanitarian cancer research. And Mack knows it would be futile to explain that the money is needed for Doc's party. Instead, he seizes the opportunity to praise the man's dogs, to flatter his skill as a

[25]   Steinbeck, *Sea of Cortez*, p. 96.
[26]   Steinbeck, *Cannery Row*, p. 88.

breeder in order to win his favor and get to the frogs. "'I bet Mack could of been president of the U.S. if he wanted", says Hazel, one the boys. "'What could he do with it if he had it?' Jones asked. 'There wouldn't be no fun in that.'"[27]

Doc too knows the difficulties in trying to tell the truth to a society that does not like the truth. Once, during a walking tour from Indiana to Florida, Doc tried answering people's questions by telling them that he walked because he wanted to see the country. But people scowled or laughed because they knew he was a liar; or else, afraid for their pigs and daughters, they told him to move on. So Doc reverted to the lie that he was making the trip on a hundred dollar bet. "Everyone liked him then and believed him. They asked him in to dinner and gave him a bed and they put up lunches for him. ... Doc still loved true things but he knew it was not a general love and it could be a very dangerous mistress."[28]

Even in the comic mode of *Cannery Row*, Steinbeck persists in the development of his constant themes. The group, in this case, is composed of Mack and the boys, and the girls at Dora's Bear Flag cafe. Like the migrants of *The Grapes of Wrath* they are individualists who join forces and become a unit to gain a cause; like the migrants they are an "outsider" group whose existence is a threat to the established social order. Of course, the serious search of the migrants for acknowledgement of their human dignity cannot be classed with the mock heroic efforts of the outcasts of Cannery Row to throw a successful party for Doc, but the similarities do exist and make us aware of Steinbeck's technical versatility. The untouchable bums and prostitutes of Cannery Row also have their leaders, Mack and Dora, who are wise to the ways of survival in a hostile world. When an influenza epidemic strikes the children of the Row, Mack and Dora know that their community, "not considered a very good financial risk", will be slighted by the doctors, and so they muster their energies and funds to tend to the sick and needy. When, perennially, the "high-minded ladies in the town demanded that dens of vice must close to protect young American manhood",[29]

[27] *Ibid.*, p. 52.
[28] *Ibid.*, pp. 64-65.
[29] *Ibid.*, pp. 90:91.

Dora knew that she need only wait a week or two before reopening the doors of her sporting house; by then the husbands of the high-minded ladies, who were also the landlords and patrons of the sporting houses, would feel the effects of the closing, and, in fact, the town would begin to feel the economic pinch when the conventions got the news and switched their reservations to more liberal towns. For much the same reasons that Mack is favored in Steinbeck's scheme — because he is the opposite of respectable success — so is Dora a heroine. She runs

a decent, clean, honest, old-fashioned sporting house where a man can take a glass of beer among friends. This is no fly-by-night clip-joint but a sturdy, virtuous club, built, maintained, and disciplined by Dora who … has through the exercise of special gifts of tact and honesty, charity and a certain realism, made herself respected by the intelligent, the learned, and the kind. And by the same token she is hated by the twisted and lascivious sisterhood of married spinsters whose husbands respect the home but don't like it very much.[30]

The reader will recall that Steinbeck's groups are apt to take one of two forms. Those bullied into existence and motivated by fear, whose members never had individual lives of their own, are doomed to extinction because their ends are unclear and because they therefore cannot take intelligent or dedicated action. Such, for example, was the nature of the vigilante groups of *In Dubious Battle* and *The Grapes of Wrath*, as opposed to the migrants, whose purposes became clear, who acted as intelligent individuals, and whose leaders sprang from the people. On these grounds, the first party for Doc is a failure because it lacks inspiration and a reason for being, because it does not enlist the cooperation of the whole community (Mack ignores all but his own boys), and, of course, because poor planning does not take into account that Doc will not be home. But the second party succeeds because everyone is united spiritually by the will to pay homage to Doc and to atone for the destruction wrought by the first party. The second party takes on a life of its own, at one moment somber and peaceful, at the next joyful and frenzied; it is unpredictable, but ultimately quite satisfied with its life. It is every bit as much fun as Steinbeck wanted it to be,

[30] *Ibid.*, pp. 9-10.

its frolicking bums and prostitutes, like satyrs and nymphs, all the while flaunting their unabashed happiness in the face of the conventional world. The description of the party is Steinbeck's humor at its best, but he does not quite let us forget the undercurrent of serious social satire, the poison in the cream puff, and he recalls it to us in the familiar biological terminology of his group man theory:

> The nature of parties has been imperfectly studied. It is, however, generally understood that a party has a pathology, that it is a kind of an individual and that it is likely to be a very perverse individual. And it is also generally understood that a party hardly ever goes the way it is planned or intended. This last, of course, excludes those dismal slave parties, whipped and controlled and dominated, given by ogreish professional hostesses. These are not parties at all but acts and demonstrations, about as spontaneous as peristalsis and as interesting as its end product.[31]

The reader may have surmised by this point that Steinbeck's biologist-hero, his philosopher-spokesman in this novel of unmanners, is Doc. Self-exiled from the competitive and sophisticated world, he prefers the company of the free-spirited and honest-passioned inhabitants of Cannery Row. By acclamation their deity, he is loved, feared and respected by them. Still, "in spite of his friendliness and his friends, Doc was a lonely and a set-apart man".[32] The complete Steinbeckian hero, Doc is a biologist, the proprietor of Western Biological Laboratory, who retreats to the tide pools to discover the microcosms of all life. His philosophical point of view is, of course, non-teleological, which leaves him free to be what he is and to accept others as they are. He is, as he puts it, "a free man", unashamed of reading sentimental poetry or listening to Claire de Lune, or, on the other hand, free to indulge a classicist taste for Bach or Gregorian chants. Religious music is often heard coming from his shaded window at night, indicating that he is with a girl. He is very kind and understanding to Dora and her girls, but he does not patronize them; we are told that "his sex life was too complicated for that".

[31] *Ibid.*, p. 114.
[32] *Ibid.*, p. 62.

Doc is deified not only because he is the advisor and consoler of every inhabitant of Cannery Row, but also because in his wisdom he provides the order that even an outcast society must have. When, unaware of the plans for the first party, he is out of town, chaos reigns. Next time, however, forewarned, he controls the event from behind the scenes, even to the extent of getting a supply of good liquor, since he knows that his "guests" will not bring enough; and he makes certain that everything breakable is removed beforehand from his laboratory. During the party, like a god pleased with the offering of his children, he sits "cross-legged on the table", smiling and tapping his fingers.[33]

Fully aware of, and deeply affected by the chaos and hypocrisies of the war, Steinbeck wrote *Cannery Row* as an attack on the seemingly respectable. The community of outcasts are the antithesis of such "respectability", and, by an ironic reversal of moral values, they become the Beauties and the Virtues. If they are funny people, it is because as civilized readers we know that such total honesty and such dedication to the instinctively right cannot exist except in fiction. But, in this case, to note the gap between the real and the fictional is also to recognize the critical commentary on the weaknesses of modern man and modern society.

THE MOON IS DOWN

Thus far in this chapter I have indicated Steinbeck's transitory threefold reactions to the war, all of which can be readily understood as expressions of his emotional positions. His expeditions to the Gulf of California and to Mexico, resulting in *Sea of Cortez* and *The Forgotten Village*, were largely induced by his determination to escape "the fear and fierceness and contagion" of the war that had begun in Europe. Then, the attack on the United States and our active involvement in the war prompted Steinbeck's conscious subordination of his hatred of men's thoughtless destruction; it was not in his nature to remain passive, and he attested to his commitment with *Bombs Away* and the series of dispatches from the frontlines.

[33]   *Ibid.*, p. 119.

Finally, not so much disillusioned with the war as with the facade of respectability that cloaked the manipulators of the war (business-men, generals, censors — men who, given the chance, would become the manipulators of the peacetime world), Steinbeck satirized, in *Cannery Row*, the values of a sick and cynical war-weary world.

But there is one work from this period which I have refrained from discussing until now because it defies classification as either a contribution to the war effort or as critical commentary on war. Oddly, *The Moon is Down* was written during the three months after the attack on Pearl Harbor and before the publication in March, 1942, of *Bombs Away*; odd because, knowing of Steinbeck's despondency over the threat of war, one might have expected his first reactions, once we were in the war, to be something more emotional and less complacent, more humane and less coldly bionomical than *The Moon is Down* appeared to be. Perhaps his tone can be accounted for by the fact that Steinbeck had just completed *Sea of Cortez* in which his view of the war from six thousand miles away, though often expressed in wryly condem-natory terms, was consistently that of the objective and analytic observer, the scientist with an air of detachment from the human side of the affair. In any case, some critics and readers condemned the book for its failure to aid the war effort, and, more vehemently, some accused Steinbeck of Nazi sympathies.[34] The objections were based in part on the fact that the book did not deal in the stereotypes of sadistic, monocled Nazis, or clever, clean-cut underground agents — types that were in increasing demand and supply in fiction during the war.

A more likely explanation of the mild furor over the novel would seem to be that Steinbeck had not yet been caught up in the "war effort", that he still retained a view of the larger issues which, for most of the public, had been obscured by the chauvinism of the times. From the perspective of peacetime it is easy to see that Steinbeck's intentions were, if not hysterically partisan, quite ap-propriately patriotic. In 1953, he commented:

[34] For a full view of the public controversy that raged over the question of Steinbeck's sympathies, see Hyman's article, and Lisca, pp. 186-188, both noted above.

The war came on, and I wrote *The Moon is Down* as a kind of celebration of the durability of democracy. I couldn't conceive that the book would be denounced. I had written of Germans as men, not supermen, and this was considered a very weak attitude to take.[35]

As for the complaint that the book lacks a humane point of view because it deals with men at war as if they were specimens in an ecological experiment, it needs only to be repeated that for Steinbeck there was no conflict between the non-teleological method of handling data (including human events) and a compassionate understanding of the human predicament. The two, in fact, are interdependent.

With hindsight, we can now appreciate that *The Moon is Down* was Steinbeck's only "serious" novel between 1939 (*The Grapes of Wrath*) and 1947 (*The Wayward Bus*), and as such it represents the most reliable link between his pre and post war fiction. As I have indicated, his other attempts to employ his dominant themes during the war years were always, in some manner and in some part, twisted to suit the special conditions of the war and his highly emotional reactions to it.

The Moon is Down does deal with one part of the war — the occupation of a small country by a powerful conquerer. But Steinbeck took special pains to universalize the situation by never specifying that the invaded country was Norway or that the invaders were Nazis. He was not naively hoping that his readers would fail to see that his models were in fact Hitler's military machine and one of its Scandinavian victims, but by being hypothetical about dates, names, and events, he hoped to reduce the effect of the book as propaganda and focus on that greater issue, "the durability of democracy". In the international conflict between the forces of democracy and the forces of totalitarianism, Steinbeck found fertile ground for his major themes, and for the first time since *Cup of Gold* they were set in land outside of his familiar American West.

The people of the small North European town, not unlike the Oklahoma farmers of *The Grapes of Wrath*, were softened by a hundred years of peace and relative economic security that left

[35]   Steinbeck, *Wings*, p. 7.

them unprepared for any sudden change, and like sluggish animals they were vulnerable to invasion and extinction: "By ten-forty-five it was all over. The town was occupied, the defenders defeated and the war finished."[36] One recalls the first unbelieving reactions of the Oklahomans as the great, bank-owned tractors rolled over their land and houses. Uncomprehending, and at first even embarrassed by not knowing how to receive the new lords of the land, the farmers stepped forward to greet the tractor drivers in order to reason with them; after all, the drivers were the sons of their friends. Similarly, in the house of Mayor Orden, there is great discussion concerning the proprieties of welcoming Colonel Lanser and his staff of conquerors. "'Should we offer them tea or a glass of wine?'" wonders the mayor's wife. "'I don't know'", answers the mayor. "'It's been so long since we conquered anybody or anybody conquered us. I don't know what is proper.'"[37]

This bewilderment and fumbling for direction are symptomatic of the society diseased by over-security, and when that society is attacked by a well-organized, well-led army with the singular purpose of conquest, there would seem to be little hope for its survival, much less its victory. But it is at this point that Steinbeck merges his theory of groups and their survival techniques with his faith in the strength of people who are grounded in long democratic traditions. The efficient invaders have shocked the complacent villagers into momentary submission, but they are mistaken in thinking that they can continue to control the will of the group. The situation is once again comparable to that of *The Grapes of Wrath*. The shocked farmers discovered brotherhood, strength, and purpose in their mutual sorrow and struggle. Most important, they were adaptable, willing to change in order to meet the new conditions of survival. And this adaptability contained the important feature of producing new leaders, whenever they were needed, to represent the common will. The villagers of *The Moon is Down*, by virtue of their tradition of freedom and democracy, manifest a similar adaptability that confounds their conquerers. After the initial confusion, they meet in secret to talk out ways of combatting the

[36] John Steinbeck, *The Moon is Down* (New York, 1942), p. 175.
[37] *Ibid.*, pp. 24-25.

superior forces of the enemy. They form "undergrounds" which in turn enlist the aid of all the people to harass the invaders through acts of sabotage that range from the simple but unsettling policy of non-fraternization with the enemy enlisted men, to "commando-type" killings of guards. That the strategy works is indicated by the hysterical outcry, by one of Colonel Lanser's increasingly nervous staff, that the flies had conquered the flypaper.

In thus depicting the defensive tactics of the invaded people, Steinbeck was illustrating not military but ecological principles. The invaders would be defeated, despite their military might, because, unlike the "free men" who voluntarily united to defend the liberty they cherished as individuals, they were "herd men" who depended for survival on the will and directives of their leaders. They were flustered by the attacks of the "underground" because neither their orders nor their rule books told them how to meet unorthodox situations; unlike the villagers, they lacked adaptability.

Colonel Lanser, for example, because he is a product of narrow totalitarian traditions, both military and intellectual, makes the crucial error of assuming that the community is predictable and controllable, that he can subject the people to his rule by issuing his orders through the office of the mayor. But Mayor Orden, even during the first numbing moments of the occupation, while he is still trying to maintain a "civilized" relationship with the conquerers, is skeptical. He tells the Colonel:

"Sir, I am of this people, and yet I don't know what they will do. Perhaps you know. Or maybe it would be different from anything you know or we know. Some people accept appointed leaders and obey them. But my people have elected me. They made me and they can unmake me. Perhaps they will if they think I have gone over to you. I just don't know."[38]

And near the end of the novel, when repeated acts of sabotage should have made it clear to them that the people will follow no leader who does not represent their will, the desperate invaders take Mayor Orden hostage for what they hope will be a guarantee against the lighting of one more fuse. "'You don't understand'",

[38] *Ibid.*, p. 36.

Orden tells Colonel Lanser, "'When I have become a hindrance to the people, they will do without me.'"[39] Then a whistle blows, indicating an explosion at the coal mine where most of the village men are forced to work under heavy guard. Again Orden speaks:

"You see, sir, nothing can change it. You will be destroyed and driven out. ... The people don't like to be conquered, sir, and so they will not be. Free men cannot start a war, but once it is started, they can fight on in defeat. Herd men, followers of a leader, cannot do that, and so it is always the herd men who win battles and the free men who win wars."[40]

I have several times offered in evidence Steinbeck's concern, in his pre-war novels, with the psychology and "biology" of groups composed of herd men and of free men. In fact, in *In Dubious Battle*, *Of Mice and Men*, and *The Grapes of Wrath*, the three novels preceding *The Moon is Down*, Steinbeck wrote extensively of the conflict between grass roots people with fervent democratic principles (the strikers, the bindlestiffs, and the migrants), and a kind of home-grown fascist (the vigilantes and the lynch mobs). It is therefore of particular importance, as an indication of the continuing development of Steinbeck's basic themes even during the early, uncertain day of the war, that *The Moon is Down* extends the group-man theory to nations and political ideologies. In the pre-war *Sea of Cortez* Steinbeck wrote in general, non-political terms about his group-man concept and his ecological findings. But after the war, in the introduction to the reissued narrative portion of the book, his observations include several noticeably partisan and political examples. To illustrate the concept that "over-integration in human groups might parallel the law in paleontology that over-armor or over-ornamentation are symptoms of decay and disappearance" (the same concept dramatized in *The Moon is Down*), Steinbeck makes this comparison:

Consider ... the Third Reich or the Politburo-controlled Soviet. The sudden removal of twenty-five key men from either system could cripple it so thoroughly that it would take a long time to recover, if it ever could. ... A too greatly integrated system or society is in danger of destruction since the removal of one unit may cripple the whole. ...

[39] *Ibid.*, p. 183.
[40] *Ibid.*, pp. 185-186.

Twenty-five key men destroyed could make the Soviet union stagger, but we could lose our congress, our president, and our general staff and nothing much would have happened. We would go right on.[41]

These ideas are a clear echo of words spoken in *The Moon is Down* by Dr. Winter (who shares with Mayor Orden Steinbeck's traditional hero role as leader-scientist-observer):

"They [the invaders] think that just because they have one leader and one head, we are all like that. They know that ten heads lopped off will destroy them, but we are a free people; we have as many heads as we have people, and in time of need leaders pop up among us like mushrooms."[42]

Beyond its value in extending these themes to more nearly universal situations, *The Moon is Down* evidences a skein of thought which Steinbeck was to lose hold of for the remainder of the war, pick up gingerly soon after the war, and finally strengthen and grasp firmly as the mainstay of a great novel — *East of Eden*. The new emphasis was on individual freedom of the will, the responsibility of each man, for the sake of reaffirming his human dignity, to choose between right and wrong. *The Moon is Down* touches on this matter of choice whenever it focuses on Mayor Orden's inner conflict between his desire to represent his people and his fear for his personal safety. In subordinating his fears, Orden recalls Socrates, in the *Apology*: "'A man who is good for anything ought not to calculate the chance of living or dying; he ought only to consider whether he is doing right or wrong.'" And later, when Colonel Lanser asks him to tell the villagers to quit their violence, Orden, knowing that the people will not listen if he does not act for their benefit, answers:

"I have no choice of living or dying, you see, sir, but — I do have a choice of how I do it. If I tell them not to fight, they will be sorry, but they will fight. If I tell them to fight, they will be glad, and I who am not a very brave man will have made them a little braver."[43]

Steinbeck had dealt often before with the human will, but in the

---

[41]   John Steinbeck, *The Log From the Sea of Cortez* (New York, 1951), pp. xlvi-xlvii.
[42]   Steinbeck, *The Moon is Down*. p. 175.
[43]   *Ibid.*, p. 185.

most important instances his concern was with the will of groups considered as units. And he had also often dealt with individual responsibility, but these cases usually emphasized the individual's responsibility towards the group he represented. Mayor Orden, it is true, is closely involved with and influenced by a group movement, but it is noteworthy that Steinbeck chose to establish Orden's victory over himself as an issue quite distinct, in its personal nature, from the victory gained by the people, *earlier*, when they decided to fight on. It is for this reason that I believe that Steinbeck's new affirmation of the importance of the individual will had its beginning in *The Moon is Down*.

Although Steinbeck did not fully or competently deal with this philosophic departure until *East of Eden*, some links in the chain of its development reappear soon after the war, and they deserve some brief comment.

TRANSITION: A REAFFIRMATION

Despite the fact that Steinbeck's productivity fell off drastically in the years immediately following the war,[44] the period may be seen as a profitable preparation for *East of Eden*, which Steinbeck began writing in 1947 and completed in 1952, the year of its publication. It was a period of combined rejection and affirmation: rejection of the materialism and predatoriness which he saw as the prevailing conditions of the post-war world, but affirmation of the individual will to survive the dangers of that world. Although Kino and Juan Chicoy, respectively the heroes of *The Pearl* and *The Wayward Bus*, win victories, their achievements are personal and in no way reflect hope that the race might follow their examples. Indeed, they are solitary, self-reliant men who either come to reject the world (Kino) or refuse to enter it (Juan), leaving it to wallow in its iniquities while they preserve their own souls. Nevertheless, herein are the seeds of

[44] During the seven years between *Cannery Row* and *East of Eden* Steinbeck published: a novel, *The Wayward Bus* (1947); a novella, *The Pearl* (1947); a pictorial travel book with Frank Capa, *A Russian Journal* (1948); an experimental and unsuccessful play, *Burning Bright* (1950); and *The Log from the Sea of Cortez* (1951).

Steinbeck's emerging emphasis on man's freedom of choice between good and evil; herein the necessary preparation for the kind of affirmation Steinbeck was to voice through several of the heroes of *East of Eden*. The following, for example, is the revelation of the patriarchal Samuel Hamilton:

"'Thou mayest rule over sin. ... *Thou mayest! Thou mayest!*' What glory! It is true that we are weak and sick and quarrelsome, but if that is all we ever were, we would, millenniums ago, have disappeared from the face of the earth. A few remnants of fossilized jawbone, some broken teeth in strata of limestone, would be the only mark man would have left of his existence in the world. But the choice, ... the choice of winning!"[45]

The Pearl is a beautifully written parable, a folk-allegory of a simple Mexican fisherman whose discovery of man's evil bears none of the fruits of glory that Samuel Hamilton was able to pluck from the "weak and sick and quarrelsome" world. Kino refers to the huge and flawless pearl he has accidentally found, as "the Pearl of the World",[46] for it comes to symbolize to him freedom from his fisherman's life of bondage to the sea. He believes it will secure entrance, through education for his child, into a dimly seen better life: "'My son will read and open books, and my son will write and will know writing. And my son will make numbers, and these things will make us free because he will know — he will know and through him we will know.'"[47]

But instead of knowing freedom, Kino gains a knowledge of the acts of greed and brutality that men will commit in order to get the pearl for the wealth it will bring. The world, like the pearl that symbolizes it, is a shining deceit, and we find that Kino cannot keep the pearl without himself becoming corrupted. The courageous and trusting Kino experiences for the first time in his life the emotions of defensive fear and suspicion, and in his blindness he courts the destruction of all he values most. His vain struggle to protect the pearl brings about the loss of his home, a spiritual estrangement from his wife, and the death of his son.

[45] John Steinbeck, *East of Eden* (New York, 1952), pp. 308-309.
[46] Before it appeared as a book and motion picture in 1947, the story was published as "The Pearl of the World" in *Woman's Home Companion*, December, 1945.
[47] John Steinbeck, *The Pearl* (New York, 1947), p. 38.

Steinbeck reminds us in the introduction to *The Pearl*, that in parables, "as with all retold tales that are in people's hearts, there are only good and bad things and black and white things".[48] This is the rationale of *The Pearl*. Kino, in his primitive simplicity, is the good; the civilized world, glittering with deceitful wealth and power, is the bad. But unlike most parables, this one does not end with good triumphing over evil. Rather, it ends with Kino's withdrawal from and rejection of society's illusory offerings. His bitter experiences finally lead him to throw the pearl back into the sea.

Samuel Hamilton and others in *East of Eden* were actually to exult in their discovery of evil, for it gave them the opportunity to examine its nuances, to exercise their separate and social wills against it, and finally, if they were strong enough, to rule over it. It is apparent, however, that when Steinbeck wrote *The Pearl*, the most he could hope for was Kino's kind of courage in confronting the forces of evil, recognizing them, and then consciously rejecting them. In the black and white allegory, good could not remain in the company of evil and still retain its identity.

The Wayward Bus marks no significant change in Steinback's view of evil in the post-war world. If anything, this is a more bitter book than *The Pearl*, more intent in its dissection of evil. But by virtue of his closer examination of several shades and varieties of evil (back on familiar California ground) Steinbeck takes another step toward the themes of *East of Eden*. Perhaps the important difference is that, whereas in the later novel he was to reincorporate the "understanding-acceptance" aspect of his non-teleological philosophy, Steinbeck has no compassion, nor even mercy, for the lost, ugly creatures of *The Wayward Bus*. In previous books, what has made Steinbeck's scientific approach more than coldly objective analysis of human specimens, has been his determination to take into account the human soul and to see human beings in important relationship to "all reality, known and unknowable". Although *The Wayward Bus* is a shocking indictment of several types of American species, it is little more than a lineup of specimens under microscopic examination; it is a weak book because it fails to attribute human qualities to human animals and because it fails to

[48]   *Ibid.*, p. 2.

involve the reader's emotions through identification and pity. Nor is it valid to defend these weaknesses on the grounds that the book is an allegory that does not require "round" characters. Even the allegorical novel, if it is to be successful as a novel, must create a convincing plot and convincing characters so that the reader may be led, by indirection, to its allegorical meaning. In *The Wayward Bus* Steinbeck overtly *tells* his meanings; his characters are explained more than they are described, and action is subordinated to such explanation.

However, despite its esthetic weaknesses, *The Wayward Bus* does approach *East of Eden* on two points of theme. First, it deals with evil as a variable and thus, although it fails to illustrate any transformations, holds out hope for the regeneration of some of its characters through an exercise of the will. Second, through its hero Juan Chicoy it touches upon some of those mystical and religious concerns that Steinbeck had not fully treated since *The Grapes of Wrath*.

Peter Lisca affords a convenient approach to the first theme by arranging the passengers on the allegorical journey aboard the wayward bus into three main groups: "the damned, those in purgatory, and the saved or elect."[49] Using this method of classification (although not necessarily placing the characters where Mr. Lisca has placed them), I find that Mr. Elliot Pritchard, his wife Bernice, and Mr. Van Brunt, belong among the damned; those in purgatory include Norma, "Pimples" Carson, Ernest Horton, Camille Oaks, and Mildred Pritchard. Only Juan is of the elect. The value of thus categorizing is to indicate the scope and variety of sins Steinbeck chose to confer upon his menagerie of lost souls, and to indicate that some among those souls still had a chance for salvation. The damned are utterly lost. Elliot Pritchard has for too long indulged in the hypocrisies of business "ethics" to begin now to be honest with others or himself. When, for a moment, he catches sight of his cruelties and rapacity, the best he can do is recoil in blame upon his wife and rape her in the dirt of a cave. Mrs. Pritchard is sexually frigid, with the result that she considers vulgar the healthy sexual appetites of others. She takes refuge from

[49]   Lisca, p. 233.

reality in ostentation and by playing an active role in women's clubs. Van Brunt's sin is lechery compounded by an outward show of puritanical virtue; his old body, twisted by infirmities, is symbolic of the sickness of his soul.

The purgatorial souls have in common youth and a vague desire, without knowledge of the means, to improve their condition. Their sins are largely visited upon them from their elders, the damned. "Pimples" Carson and Norma are late adolescents who work for Juan, "Pimples" as a mechanic and Norma as a waitress in the lunchroom. "Pimples" comes by his acne through his faith in candy bar commericals that promise energy when he needs it most. But both feed their souls excessively on commercial offers of success and beauty; both have their thinking warped by the illusions garnered from motion pictures, and Norma lives in the dream that Clark Gable will someday "discover" her and rescue her from the ignominy of small town waitresshood. One might say that they are the victims of the world that Mr. Pritchard symbolizes — a world of "business first" that manufactures illusions for the ignorant and meek. Nevertheless, Steinbeck indicates that they are not yet damned, that there is still some hope for their salvation. While they take no real step forward, they do exhibit qualities that might eventually provide them with some dignity and self-hood. "Pimples", for example, takes pride in his work as a mechanic, and he may yet, under the instruction of Juan, become one of Steinbeck's men of skill in the tradition of Slim from *Of Mice and Men* and Al from *The Grapes of Wrath*. And Norma, we find, although she may never reach the wisdom and virtue of Dora, the Madame of *Cannery Row*, may, under the tutelage of Camille Oaks, become a realistic and honest prostitute.

Ernest Horton and Camille Oaks have committed the sin of complicity; their place in purgatory, however, offers them the opportunity to reject the society which they both abhor but support by accepting despicable roles in it. Horton is a salesman of practical jokes, including one "hot" item called the "Little Wonder Artificial Sore Foot". He thus contributes to the spiritual delinquency of the world. Camille is a stripper whose speciality is appearing in the nude at stag parties attended by Mr. Pritchard's ilk. Nevertheless, there is hope for Ernest and Camille because they cherish no illusions about their base professions. Ernest, in fact, when he gives the name of "high-class blackmail" to what Pritchard had preferred to consider ethical business, is responsible for a small tear in Mr. Pritchard's veil of illusion. Camille would prefer the uncomplicated life of a middle class housewife but since, for reasons beyond her control, she exudes sex, she knows that her dream is impossible. She therefore accepts her fate with stoical courage and takes the more practical of two evil choices: "She didn't understand stags or what satisfaction the men got out of them, but there they were, and she made fifty dollars for taking off her clothes and that was better than having them torn off in an office."[50] When Ernest and Camille agree without pretense or shame to ally themselves in a love affair, the reader is asked to see their honest acceptance of the healthy sex drive as a symbolic rejection of one of society's major hypocrisies, and thus, for the pair, as a step upwards out of purgatory.

Mildred, the Pritchards' twenty-one year old only child, has the hardest path to follow out of purgatory but perhaps the best chance for salvation. Her handicap has been her parents, who have all but smothered her in their values, but, while she has retained some finishing school snobbishness, she has rebelled against her parents' orthodoxies even before she appears in the novel. More than any other character, she *acts* to assure her salvation. Leaving her bewildered parents to wonder where they have gone wrong in her upbringing, she searches out Juan in an abandoned barn and there seduces him — a symbolic act of regeneration for her since Juan represents the "complete man", in union with whom "incomplete modern woman" can find fulfillment.

There, except for Juan Chicoy, the "elect" driver, are the passengers of the bus. All, depending upon the kind and extent of their sins, are on some level of damnation; none achieves absolution or salvation during the course of the journey; a few, if they continue to purge their souls of the influence of unnatural social conventions, may hope for regeneration.

In considering Juan Chicoy, I must also consider the novel's other theme, manifest in Steinbeck's renewed interest in the religious and

[50] John Steinbeck, *The Wayward Bus* (New York, 1947), pp. 109-110.

mystical elements of life. First of all, Juan is "elect" among the damned because he is, as I have said, the novel's only complete "man", and, in Steinbeck's terms, "there aren't very many of them in the world, as everyone finds out sooner or later".[51] The virtues of Juan's manhood are drawn in direct contrast to the total of evil embodied in the other characters of *The Wayward Bus*: not coincidentally these are the virtues previously contained in most of Steinbeck's typical heroes. Juan is as skilled with mechanical things ("his hands moved with speed and precision"[52]) as he is with women ("he felt a glow of pleasure knowing that he could take this girl Mildred and twist her and outrage her if he wanted to."[53]) He is not only the driver of the bus, he is the leader of its passengers. While they bicker and worry over a series of mishaps during the journey, Juan decides which roads to take and organizes the group's energies to get the bus out of the mud. Self-sufficient, he can also be methodical and aloof in dealing with his wards; at one point, disgusted with their selfishness and dishonesty, he temporarily leaves them to their helplessness. While he does not have the patience or sympathy of Doc Burton or Jim Casy, he does share their ecological view of life; he sees "each thing in relation to the other".[54]

Also like Jim Casy, Juan has abandoned traditional, orthodox religion for one of his own making — a strange combination of pagan fetishism backed up by practical modern instruments to ward off society's evils:

Hanging from the top of the windshield were the penates: a baby's shoe — that's for protection, for the stumbling feet of a baby require the constant caution and aid of God; and a tiny boxing glove — and that's for power ... , the power of person as responsible and proud individual. ... Also ... a little plastic kewpie doll for the pleasures of the flesh and of the eye, of the nose, of the ear.[55]

And on top of the dashboard:

[51] *Ibid.*, p. 6.
[52] *Ibid.*, p. 15.
[53] *Ibid.*, p. 83.
[54] *Ibid.*, p. 35.
[55] *Ibid.*, pp. 19-20.

A small metal Virgin of Guadalupe ... , Juan Chicoy's connection with eternity. It had little to do with religion as connected with the church and dogma, and much to do with religion as memory and feeling.[56]

Uneasy without these symbols, Juan also has faith in more practical symbols. He keeps within reach a bottle of whiskey, bandage, smelling salts, and a revolver.

In this allegory of the broken down bus of the world, Juan plays the role of savior. He may have once struggled in the world as one of its passengers, but he comes to the novel *after* he has mastered the conditions of life in which the others are still trapped. Not only does he reject their evil ways but, since he retains only the best of the civilized world (his skill as a craftsman) and the best of the primitive, instinctive world of the past (his religion of "memory and feeling"), he is also immune to those evils. Juan is godlike also in mien. He appears to Mildred, for example, as a kind of presence, his appeal to her going beyond mere sexuality: "There was something in this dark man with his strange warm eyes that moved her. She felt drawn to him. She wanted to attract his attention, his special attention, to herself."[57] Perhaps an unneccessary touch, nevertheless significant, is the fact that Juan's initials, like Jim Casy's, are J.C. God-like, Juan *condescends* to drive the passengers through dangerous floods and along treacherous roads. But he reserves the right to abandon them when they misbehave. Finally, still in anger over their pettiness and hypocrisies, Juan returns to the bus to drive it further along on its painful journey.

In *The Wayward Bus* Steinbeck dwelt more on the shapes of evil than on man's struggle to master them. He offered some vague hope for salvation to a few souls who might outrun evil, but he did not illustrate the greater nobility of man standing his ground and gaining personal, if tragic, victory. The beauty and exaltation of such victory was to come in *East of Eden*.

The years between 1941 and 1952 were for Steinbeck, even considering some gaps, highly productive.[58] But the fact must stand

[56]   *Ibid.*, p. 21.
[57]   *Ibid.*, p. 82.
[58]   Besides the works already mentioned, Steinbeck turned out two motion picture scripts — *The Red Pony* and *Viva Zapata* — which have become film classics.

that his work of this period was qualitatively inferior to what had come before. This is not to say that all of his work was failure. Far from it. *Cannery Row* must be placed high in the ranks of great satire; *The Moon is Down* is a rare fictional celebration of the spirit of democracy; and even the war journalism contains vivid pictures of the souls of men threatened with the loss of identity. Steinbeck sometimes despaired of the world when man seemed bent on his own destruction, but equally as often his vision was of man triumphant, and his writings then, as I have tried to show, were portentous of the powerful affirmations of *East of Eden*. It is fitting and significant that his last published work before that novel was *The Log from the Sea of Cortez*. This act in itself was a reaffirmation of the principles he had explicitly set forth ten years earlier.

VIII

EAST OF EDEN: "THOU MAYEST"

"If *East of Eden* isn't good, then I've been wasting my time. It has in it everything I have been able to learn about my art or craft or profession in all these years."[1]

Steinbeck had learned well the lessons of the years: *East of Eden* is his most accomplished work of craftsmanship. And, beyond craftsmanship, Steinbeck's creation of the novel was an act of love, a passionately moral declaration of his vision of the human condition: "Pain and excitement are in it, and feeling good or bad and evil thoughts and good thoughts — the pleasure of design and some despair and the indescribable joy of creation."[2]

East of Eden is a long book (four parts, six hundred pages) and a complex book (a dozen major characters spanning almost three generations). For these reasons, and because the novel has been criticized as structurally weak, I shall consider its structure separately before taking up its themes — although I hope to also show how Steinbeck has carefully welded theme to structure.

When the book first appeared, in September of 1952, most reviewers praised it highly.[3] Most had little to say about the novel's technique and structure, concentrating instead on the fast pace of its action, the beauty of its narrative, and the power of its message. It seems fair to say that these reviewers implied their approval of

[1] John Steinbeck, quoted in Bernard Kale, "The Author", *Saturday Review* XXXV (September 20, 1952), 11.

[2] John Steinbeck, in the Dedication to Pascal Covici, *East of Eden* (New York, 1952).

[3] Among those favorably reviewing *East of Eden* were: Joseph Wood Krutch for the *New York Herald Tribune*, Mark Schorer for *The New York Times*, and Mme. Claude-Edmonde Magny for *Perspectives, USA*.

the novel's structural soundness when they stressed their absorption in its plot, language, and theme. At least, there seems to have been no flaw in structure important enough to make them turn their practiced critical senses from what they agreed was a well told story involving timeless human values — perhaps, after all, the two true elements of great fiction. Typical of critical reaction was Joseph Wood Krutch's comment:

> The whole ramifying narrative holds the attention to an extraordinary degree throughout the six hundred long pages. ... Never, I think, not even in The *Grapes of Wrath*, has he exhibited such a grip upon himself and upon his material. ... There is seriousness as well as violence; passion rather than sentimentality.[4]

And even when Mr. Krutch points to a disturbing tendency of the characters to become too obviously symbolic, during the early part of the novel, he admits it only as a minor flaw:

> This awkwardness ... becomes less and less noticeable as the story proceeds. Whether that is because Mr. Steinbeck learns better how to fuse the individual and the symbol or because the reader comes to accept his method I am not sure. But in any event it is not because the symbolic intention becomes any less clear or important.[5]

The one critic who sees *East of Eden* as a total failure — structurally because Steinbeck failed "to impose an order on his diverse materials",[6] and philosophically because the weak structure cannot bear the burden of a complicated moral philosophy — is Peter Lisca, who has otherwise been Steinbeck's major critical defender and has championed the much needed re-evaluation of his work. Since I disagree with Mr. Lisca's conclusions about the novel, I should like to investigate them in some detail.

Mr. Lisca first complains about Steinbeck's "agglutination of materials", by which he means that the novel unnaturally forces together the story of the fictional Trask family with "an accurate,

---

[4] Joseph Wood Krutch, "John Steinbeck's Dramatic Tale of Three Generations", *New York Herald Tribune Book Review*, September 21, 1952, p. 1.
[5] *Ibid.*
[6] Peter Lisca, *The Wide World of John Steinbeck* (New Brunswick, N. J., 1958), p. 263.

factual account of Steinbeck's own maternal family, the Hamiltons".[7] Lisca supplies substantial evidence, from the novel's first
draft and from letters Steinbeck wrote in 1948, that the book was
originally intended as a family history written for Steinbeck's sons
so they could someday share in their father's traditions. But at some
time "as late as March of 1949" these plans were changed:

> Somewhere in the early stages of this family saga ... Steinbeck introduced
> a fictional family, the Trasks, and he soon found himself at the mercy of
> his materials. The importance of the Trask family in the novel grew until
> the author realized that he had a far different book on his hands from
> what he had originally conceived, one which centered on the Trasks and
> not on the Hamiltons. ... By this time, however, the two families were
> inextricably entangled, and the author decided to keep them that way. ..."[8]

There is no reason to doubt what Lisca has shown about Steinbeck's
original intentions. But several facts stand out to indicate that
Steinbeck was never "at the mercy of his materials" and that the
final version of the novel was a competently controlled work of art.
First of all, the book was five years in the making, but Mr. Lisca
provides evidence solely from the events of the first two years for
his contention that "Steinbeck failed to achieve fictional concentration". To those two years we can logically trace only the
germ of the novel; as Mr. Lisca himself points out, the bulk of
Steinbeck's work on the book took place during the next three
years, during which time, also, Steinbeck changed the title from
"Salinas Valley" to *East of Eden*.

Secondly, the Trask family did not just happen in and take over
the novel; nor is it true that haphazardly included autobiographical
data about the Hamiltons results in "shifts back and forth" between
the families "with no apparent purpose or method".[9] The co-
existent roles of the two families is in fact made clear as early as the
second chapter of the novel when Steinbeck introduces both Samuel
Hamilton and Adam Trask and indicates how their relationship
will become an essential part of the novel's greater scheme. Chapter
One, a pertinent geographical description of the Salinas Valley and

[7] *Ibid.*, p. 262.
[8] *Ibid.*, pp. 262-263.
[9] *Ibid.*, p. 266.

a brief history of the races that have come to it and passed out of it, ends with the coming of the Americans. Chapter Two then focuses on two of several possible types of American settlers. The first type, represented by Samuel Hamilton, is poor and destined to remain poor because it lacks a talent for making money and because without money it can never afford the richer land of the valley. The second type, represented by Adam Trask, "having sold out somewhere else, arrived with money to start a new life" by buying good land and cultivating it carefully.[10] Both types, however, have certain qualities in common:

> Because they trusted themselves and respected themselves as individuals, because they knew beyond doubt that they were valuable and potentially moral units — because of this they could give God their own courage and dignity and then receive it back.[11]

It is true that the Trasks, as the novel's central characters, come to take precedence over the Hamiltons. But this fact can no more be used to criticize the novel's structure than, for example, the dominance of the Joads over the other migrant families could be used to illustrate a distraction from the main theme of *The Grapes of Wrath*. As with that novel, *East of Eden* focuses on one family as a microcosm but is meant to represent all mankind. "A great and lasting story is about everyone or it will not last",[12] wrote Steinbeck. The Hamilton family — Samuel, Liza, and their half dozen children of diverse personality — is Steinbeck's device for giving breadth and depth to the microcosmic adventures of Adam Trask and his two sons. The importance to the novel's structure of the intertwining relationship between the two families may be illustrated by two examples. First, the sections of the book involving the Hamiltons are used in a way similar to the inter-chapters of *The Grapes of Wrath* — either to reflect and generalize action that has occurred, or to signal action that is to come. Thus, Part Three of *East of Eden* ends with the suicide of Tom Hamilton because he was incapable of bearing the burden of guilt for his sister's death. Section Four then returns to the Trasks, and in particular to Caleb

[10] Steinbeck, *East of Eden*, p. 13.
[11] *Ibid.*, p. 12.
[12] *Ibid.*, p. 270.

Trask who since his boyhood has to contend with an inordinate share of evil within himself; he now must face the responsibility for the deaths of his brother and father. Steinbeck's thesis that a man may free himself of his past and conquer evil is pointedly emphasized when, in clear contrast with Tom Hamilton's act of desperation, Caleb affirms the value of life by accepting the Biblical prophesy that "Thou mayest rule over sin".

The activities of the Hamilton family also serve, again in the manner of "inter-chapters", as a broad backdrop on which to paint the geographical, social and cultural conditions of the Salinas Valley and nineteenth century California. Chapter Fourteen, for example, is primarily about Samuel's daughter Olive, who, because she is a schoolteacher, is used to symbolize the whole cultural milieu of the fermenting West:

In the country the repository of art and science was the school, and the schoolteacher shielded and carried the torch of learning and beauty. The schoolhouse was the meeting place for music, for debate. The polls were set in the schoolhouse for elections. Social life, whether it was the crowning of a May queen, the eulogy to a dead president, or an all-night dance, could be held nowhere else. And the teacher was not only an intellectual paragon and a social leader, but also the matrimonial catch of the countryside.[13]

This passage and many others like it are always given greater reality through Steinbeck's device of linking the events with individual members of the Hamilton family. It is the same structural device which I have already described in my chapter on *The Grapes of Wrath* and which Steinbeck explained in the Preface to *The Forgotten Village*: "From association with this little personalized group, the larger conclusion concerning the racial group could be drawn with something like participation." The reader comes to know the Hamiltons intimately, and thus he comes also to know what larger conditions and principles they symbolize.

What seems to have bothered Mr. Lisca more than the "peripheral contact" between the two families, and more than the Hamiltons' "lack of purpose" in the novel, is Steinbeck's use of what Lisca calls the "autobiographical 'I'". The objection is based

[13] *Ibid.*, p. 147.

largely on the fact that most of the novel is about events which Steinbeck "not only could not have witnessed, but could not even have heard about".[14] This observation brings us back to the fallacy I earlier pointed out in Mr. Lisca's approach: his insistence upon interpreting the novel on the basis of what he learned about Steinbeck's original intentions makes it almost impossible for him to consider the book as *fiction* instead of as autobiography. Mr. Lisca makes too much of the fact that Steinbeck "appears sporadically in the novel as the narrator 'I', as 'me', and as 'John'".[15] Steinbeck's shifting point of view is really quite legitimate. Usually speaking with the voice of omniscience, Steinbeck shifts to the role of a first-person observer only when the action in some way involves the second or third generation of Hamiltons. At this point young "John" is himself a minor character who serves to provide a unique perspective by telling the story of his grandfather Samuel, and of his aunts and uncles, from the viewpoint of a child. Steinbeck as author never intrudes upon Steinbeck as character; the focus is consistently on the elder Hamiltons in their relation to the Trasks.

As a final bit of evidence to support my contention that there is no reason to read *East of Eden* as anything but fiction, here are the words of the narrator early in the novel: "I must depend on hearsay, on old photographs, on stories told, and on memories which are hazy and mixed with fable in trying to tell you about the Hamiltons."[16] Now these are the words of a first-person narrator whom, at this point in the novel, we know only as "I". But even if he were to identify himself as a character by the name of John Steinbeck (and this never happens in any manner so direct as to intrude upon the very fluid narrative), the reader would have been prepared by his words about the source of his material — "hearsay", "stories told", "memories" — for the stuff of fiction.

That Steinbeck had complete control over the structure of *East of Eden* becomes even more certain when we examine the closely woven fabric that composes the novel's thematic design. Taking his cue, as the title suggests, from the Biblical account of the human

[14] Lisca, p. 266.
[15] *Ibid.*, p. 262.
[16] Steinbeck, *East of Eden*, p. 8.

condition after man was driven from Eden, Steinbeck invests the
novel with its dominant motif out of which emanate several
subsidiary but linking theses. That primary motif may itself be
seen in two parts. First, as it describes the human condition:

Humans are caught — in their lives, in their thoughts, in their hungers
and ambitions, in their avarice and cruelty, and in their kindness and
generosity too — in a net of good and evil. I think this is the only story
we have and that it occurs on all levels of feeling and intelligence. Virtue
and vice were warp and woof of our first consciousness, and they will be
the fabric of our last, and this despite any changes we may impose on
field and river and mountain, on economy and manners. There is no
other story. A man, after he has brushed off the dust and chips of his
life, will have left only the hard, clean questions: Was it good or was it
evil? Have I done well — or ill?[17]

Second, as it describes the chance given to man to choose between
good and evil. This part of the proposition is explained by Lee, the
Trasks' educated Chinese servant, whose role as Steinbeck's spokesman I will later discuss in greater detail. At this point, however, it
is significant to know as background that Lee has long accepted the
situation of man's fall from grace into a "net of good and evil";
Lee is now concerned with man's potential for extricating himself
from that net. He has advanced as far as determining that the
center of the problem lies in the interpretation of the fourth chapter
of Genesis, where the Lord rejects Cain's gift: "And Cain was very
wroth, and his countenance fell. And the Lord said unto Cain,
' ... If thou doest well, shalt thou not be accepted? And if thou
doest not well, sin lieth at the door. And unto thee shall be his
desire, and thou shalt rule over him.'" The problem then turns
specifically on which of three possible interpretations of "thou shalt
rule over him [sin]" is the most meaningful. Lee turns the problem
over to a venerable (if unique) group of Chinese and Hebrew
scholars whose decision Lee (and Steinbeck) abides by. Lee
explains it this way:

"The American Standard translation *orders* men to triumph over sin,
and you can call sin ignorance. The King James translation makes a
promise in 'Thou shalt,' meaning that men will surely triumph over sin.

---

[17] *Ibid.*, p. 413.

But the Hebrew word, the word *timshel* — 'Thou mayest' — that gives a choice. ... There are many millions in their sects and churches who feel the order, 'Do thou', and throw their weight into obedience. And there are millions more who feel predestination in 'Thou shalt'. Nothing they may do can interfere with what will be. But 'Thou mayest'! Why, that makes a man great, that gives him stature with the gods, for in his weakness and his filth and his murder of his brother he has still the great choice. He can choose his course and fight it through and win." Lee's voice was a chant of triumph.[18]

Although this special interpretation of the Cain and Abel story ("the only story we have") is the narrative and thematic core in all of *East of Eden*'s three generations, the novel does not rely upon a simple repetition of Steinbeck's proposition that man in his weakness may still conquer himself. Because good and evil are absolutes and self-perpetuating in this scheme, and because, inherent in the idea that man is a free agent, there is the possibility that man will choose "Thou mayest not" as easily and as often as he chooses "Thou mayest", the response of each individual in each succeeding generation will never coincide. And, although the sons of each generation are faced with the same contest between good and evil in themselves as faced their fathers, their destinies are their own; they are not victimized by hereditary traits of evil — in other words, the sins of the fathers are *not* visited upon the sons. Steinbeck was therefore able to tell the story of three generations within the framework of the one imposing theme of human guilt, but since his characters were free to react variously to the human condition Steinbeck was also able to offer his readers a pattern of subsidiary themes based upon his observation of how different type-individuals weather that struggle with guilt.

This pattern of dominant and subsidiary themes may be seen clearly by tracing some of the main lines of the novel's plot. The bulk of the plot is about two generations of Trasks: the brothers Adam and Charles, and Adam's twin sons, Aaron and Caleb. Each pair of brothers re-enacts the Cain-Abel relationship, symbolized by the offering of gifts to their fathers and the fathers' rejection of the gifts in the cases of Charles and Caleb; the rejected then react in jealous violence against their brothers. It is an in-

18   *Ibid.*, p. 303.

teresting part of Steinbeck's scheme that in each case the rejected brother is the one with the greater natural inclination towards violence (thus his rejection is also a provocation), and is also the one with greater love for his father (thus implying the urgent need of the Cain-figure to "do well" in order to gain acceptance). Steinbeck's point in all this is to emphasize the larger importance of the Cain role in the history of mankind. Adam and Aaron (the Abels), inherently good, never know the bitterness of rejection and therefore never bear the burden of guilt for the sin of revenge. Exempt from the necessity of struggling to overcome baseness of character, their function in the novel is primarily to illustrate the way in which innocence eventually must come to know evil. It is for Charles and Caleb (the Cains) to make what they will of their guilt. They are put to the test to see whether they can rule over sin. Lee speaks explicitly to this point in conversation with Samuel Hamilton:

The greatest terror a child can have is that he is not loved, and rejection is the hell he fears. ... With rejection comes anger, and with anger some kind of crime in revenge for the rejection, and with the crime guilt — and there is the story of mankind. ...
One child, refused the love he craves, kicks the cat and hides his secret guilt; and another steals so that money will make him loved; and a third conquers the world — and always the guilt and revenge and more guilt. ... therefore I think this old and terrible story is important because it is a chart of the soul — the secret, rejected, guilty soul.[19]

And to Samuel's suggestion that Cain "got the dirty end of the stick", Lee reminds him that Cain lived to have children and that we are Cain's children.

The subsidiary themes, which grow out of this repeated dominant theme of rejection-revenge-guilt, come into play at those points where Charles and Caleb exercise their freedom of choice. Charles chooses to languish in self-pity; instead of laboring to rid himself of the sorrow of rejection and the sin of revenge he retreats to his farm where he labors with no hope, to no end. He dies, rich in dollar wealth, alone and unmourned. His fate is similar to Muley Graves', the unrepresentative farmer of *The Grapes of Wrath*, whose extinc-

[19]   *Ibid.*, pp. 270-271.

tion was a certainty because he could not accept conditions as they were or adapt to new conditions. Charles, although plagued with inner, spiritual, instead of outer, natural woes, loses his chance to triumph over himself because he sulks over what he mistakenly believes is his unchangeable fate, when what he should be doing is discarding the mold of his past and planning his future. Caleb too is fearful that his fate is fixed, that he has inherited the blood of his mother, a whore and murderess. Guilt-ridden over the death of his brother and his father's subsequent stroke, he considers suicide. But Lee brings him about by accusing him of self-indulgent pity, and then, in a softer, explanatory tone, helps him to put store in the value of living by giving him a sense of the promise of *timshel*:

"I thought that once an angry and disgusted God poured molten fire from a crucible to destroy or purify his little handiwork of mud.
"I thought I had inherited both the scars of the fire and the impurities which made the fire necessary — all inherited, I thought. ...
"Maybe you'll come to know that every man in every generation is refired."[20]

It is in the scheme of existence, Steinbeck was saying, that mankind is involved in the flux of good and evil. But while one man, out of laziness or weakness, resigns himself to being condemned, another will bear the mark of Cain as a symbol of hope. Steinbeck, in fact, puts heavy emphasis upon that part of the Cain-Abel story where Cain complains that his punishment is too great, that "everyone that findeth me shall slay me", and the Lord puts His mark upon him and answers, "Whosoever slayeth Cain, vengeance shall be taken on him sevenfold." And through Lee, Steinbeck explains: "'Cain bore the mark not to destroy him but to save him. ... It was a preserving mark.'"[21]

In discussing *East of Eden* thus far I have only tried to hint at its relationship to the three basic themes proposed in this study as the philosophical foundation of Steinbeck's novels. A direct examination of those themes as they work within this important novel will nearly complete my proposition that Steinbeck's thematic

[20] *Ibid.*, p. 600.
[21] *Ibid.*, p. 270.

development has been consistent. *East of Eden* is, in fact, the apex of that development.

It will be profitable to see how the Cain-Abel story is naturally compatible with Steinbeck's three-sided thematic scheme. Just as the first theme in the pattern assumes that each man searches for and finally creates a god-head that satisfies his personal religious need, so is such a search and discovery at the heart of *East of Eden's* interpretation of the sixteen verses from Genesis. The novel, as the Cain-Abel story itself, implies that man's deepest yearning is to know the nature of the God who has sent him to dwell in the vale of tears beyond Eden. If man can know whether God is vengeful, demanding, forgiving, or detached, then he can also know where he stands in God's universal plan. And Steinbeck's second theme, concerning man's dual existence as a group animal and as an individual, implies by its nature the question ("Am I my brother's keeper?") asked by Cain to determine what should be his relation to his fellow creatures. Finally, Steinbeck's non-teleological view of life, his "is" philosophy of "understanding-acceptance", emerges in *East of Eden* as the central idea behind the affirmation of *timshel*. For non-teleology assumes that man is capable of seeing his place in the universe and then taking intelligent action to improve his lot. But let us examine these themes, in detail, as they work in the novel.

For most of the minor characters of the novel there exists no problem of finding a personally satisfying god, and of course they are therefore able to create for themselves fairly stable worlds uncomplicated by the questions of identity which are the source of conflict in the novel's more complex characters. These lesser characters often choose anthropomorphic gods who serve to illumine their creators' personalities. Steinbeck writes about Adam Trask's mother, for example, in a tone of light-hearted spoofing: A humorless woman, she "used religion as a therapy for the ills of the world and of herself, and she changed the religion to fit the ill". Believing her husband dead in the war she adopts a theosophy to communicate with him. But when he returns, with just enough gonorrhea to transmit to his wife, she must "cast about for some new unhappiness. ... Her god of communication became a god of vengeance — to her the most satisfactory deity she had devised so far. ... Her new god was an expert in punishment. He demanded of her a sacrifice." With "proper egotistical humility", she sacrifices herself by holding her head under the water of a shallow pond. "This required great will power."[22]

Liza Hamilton, Samuel's wife, also chooses an anthropomorphic god, but her deity, if demanding, is not vengeful since Liza herself is not. A firm, strong-willed woman in the pioneer-puritan tradition, she is admired and treated kindly by Steinbeck:

> Liza was a good plain cook, and her house ... was brushed and pummeled and washed. Bearing her children did not hold her back very much — two weeks at the most she had to be careful. ...
> Liza had a finely developed sense of sin. Idleness was a sin, and card playing which was a kind of idleness to her. ...
> She frightened her grandchildren because she had no weakness. She suffered bravely and uncomplainingly through life, convinced that that was the way her God wanted everyone to live. She felt that rewards came later.[23]

Two hundred fifty pages after this description, Liza's uncomplicated faith appears as a significant contrast to the troublesome questions of Biblical interpretation that arise during one of the conversations between Lee, Samuel, and Adam. In the midst of their frustrating probing, Lee suddenly asks: "'How does Mrs. Hamilton feel about the paradoxes of the Bible?'" And Samuel answers: "'Why, she does not feel anything because she does not admit they are there.'"[24]

Among others whose faith is come by easily may be included such diverse personalities as Olive Hamilton and Joe Valery. Olive's theology "was a curious mixture of Irish fairies and an Old Testament Jehovah whom in her later life she confused with her father. Heaven was to her a nice home ranch inhabited by her dead relatives. She obliterated frustrating external realities by refusing to believe in them."[25] Joe Valery, the pimp at Kate's whorehouse, is a petty thief and blackmailer who has developed a "fine stable of hates" as protection against a hostile world, the only kind of world he is capable of seeing. Joe's religion combines this protective

---

[22]   *Ibid.*, p. 15.
[23]   *Ibid.*, pp. 11-12.
[24]   *Ibid.*, p. 269.
[25]   *Ibid.*, pp. 149-150.

hatred with self-worship, "a gentle protective love for Joe. He comforted and flattered and cherished Joe." And his "religion" even has a dogma, "a lonely set of rules" among which the most prominent is: "Put your faith in dough. Everybody wants it. Everybody will sell out for it."[26]

Steinbeck's assumption that individuals will often seek satisfaction for their religious cravings in the most unconventional ways and in the most unorthodox places, leads him to investigate two sturdy institutions usually considered incongruous. But Steinbeck manages, with kindness, to equate them as providers of solace for the lonely and as brighteners of the spirit for the sad:

> The church and the whorehouse arrived in the Far West simultaneously. And each would have been horrified to think it was a different facet of the same thing. But surely they were both intended to accomplish the same thing: the singing, the devotion, the poetry of the churches took a man out of his bleakness for a time, and so did the brothels.[27]

Just as various sects existed to cater to the individual appetites of church-going souls, so the brothels of Salinas varied in what each offered to its devotees. For the bacchantes there was Jenny's sacrament of "a good laugh and a poke in the ribs". But if "the sweet world-sadness close to tears crept out of your immutable loneliness", you went to the Nigger, "a handsome, austere woman with snow-white hair and a dark and awful dignity. ... She conducted her house like a cathedral dedicated to a sad but erect Priapus."[28] And for those who needed the comfort of a mother-goddess there was Faye's. "Faye was the motherly type, big-breasted, big-hipped, and warm. She was a bosom to cry on, a soother and a stroker."[29]

Steinbeck offers Cathy Trask as an extreme contrast to these big-hearted whores, to those who seek the blessings of conventional religious forms, and to those major characters of the novel whose quests for moral direction become complex tasks requiring conscious efforts of the will. All but Cathy have some potential, no matter how vague or unrealized, for good. But Cathy is a mental

[26] *Ibid.*, p. 501.
[27] *Ibid.*, p. 217.
[28] *Ibid.*, p. 220.
[29] *Ibid.*

and psychic monster, born with a "malformed soul ..., without kindness or the potential of conscience".[30] Even in her childhood Cathy knows that "nearly everyone in the world has appetites and impulses, trigger emotions, islands of selfishness, lusts just beneath the surface",[31] and she uses her knowledge cunningly for her own gain, watching gleefully the distress of her victims. Cathy deceives, tortures, murders without remorse; her "religion" is pure Satanism ("There was a time when a girl like Cathy would have been called possessed by the devil".[32]) When, after deviously destroying the trusting Faye, Cathy (now Kate) takes over the brothel, she caters to that part of man which is vicious and depraved. " 'The evil and ugly, the distorted and slimy, the worst things humans can think up are for sale there. ... Kate takes the fresh and young and beautiful and so maims them that they can never be whole again."[33]

Kate is also the link to Steinbeck's thesis that evil is not inherited, that man may, despite the history of his blood, choose to walk the path of righteousness. The twins, Aaron and Caleb, are Kate's sons, but they are not the inheritors of her depravity. Aaron is in fact his mother's opposite number: he cannot conceive of evil. When he finds out that his mother is a prostitute, he runs, not from that fact as such, but from the knowledge that there is a force alien to good. Caleb, as we have seen, is a blend of good and evil. He faces his mother in order to free himself of the lingering doubt that his destiny has been shaped by an accident of genetic circumstances. When he sees that Kate takes pleasure in her wickedness he knows that his own conscience-disturbing acts of evil are independent of the influence of her warped soul:

Cal said, "I was afraid I had you in me."

"You have", said Kate.

"No, I haven't. I'm my own. I don't have to be you. ... If I'm mean, it's my own mean."[34]

Now on this note I return to Lee and to Samuel Hamilton who,

[30] *Ibid.*, p. 72.
[31] *Ibid.*, p. 75.
[32] *Ibid.*
[33] *Ibid.*, p. 306.
[34] *Ibid.*, p. 466.

as I have indicated, are the novel's most explicit voices for Steinbeck's belief that the individual may choose between good and evil. But in considering these two men it is also necessary to turn to the second and third of Steinbeck's major themes since, in *East of Eden*, those themes are linked with Lee's and Samuel's affirmations of faith in the individual's ability to triumph over himself.

In my discussions of *The Moon is Down* and *The Wayward Bus* I pointed to the way in which Steinbeck's group-man theme was placing more and more emphasis on the individual within the group who, in the role of Steinbeck's hero, was dedicated to mankind but superior to the mass of men as such. One can, in fact, trace this development as far back as *In Dubious Battle* (Doc Burton) and *The Grapes of Wrath* (Jim Casy and Tom Joad). But in *East of Eden* the evolutionary apex is reached and the virtues of individual man are lauded almost to the detriment of group man. This does not mean that Steinbeck or his heroes have abandoned mankind, as symbolized by the group. Rather, Steinbeck's very thesis that man has potential for overcoming evil indicates that his concern for humanity is as active as ever. The difference is that responsibility for salvation is now put wholly upon the individual. This fact is implicit in *East of Eden* in Steinbeck's technique of examining the responses to the "never-ending contest in ourselves of good and evil" of a great number and variety of individuals. And in one section of the book, introductory to where Adam Trask becomes engaged in that contest, Steinbeck is explicit in his proposition:

Our species is the only creative species, and it has only one creative instrument, the individual mind and spirit of a man. Nothing was ever created by two men. There are no good collaborations, whether in music, in art, in poetry, in mathematics, in philosophy. Once the miracle of creation has taken place, the group can build and extend it, but the group never invents anything. The preciousness lies in the lonely mind of a man.[35]

These words are almost identical with what Steinbeck had written a year earlier in the introduction to *The Log From the Sea of Cortez*: "There is no creative unit in the human save the individual working alone. ... The creative principle is a lonely and an individual

[35] *Ibid.*, p. 132.

matter."[36] The fact that Steinbeck included this observation only in the later edition of *Sea of Cortez* is further evidence for my contention that his emphasis on the individual was a significant new twist to his group man theme.

Unlike Doc Burton, Jim Casy, or Mayor Orden, Lee and Samuel are not associated with any identifiable social group (unless it be mankind itself, for which the Trask family is the microcosm). Nevertheless, Steinbeck casts them in the roles of his heroes — philosophical men who view their own lives and the lives of others with scientific detachment tempered by understanding and compassion. Both are "outsiders", though respected and loved by those whose positions in society are conventional. Lee, for example, by far the best educated and most skillful character in the novel, is content to play humble Chinese servant, talk pidgin, and wear a queue, because that is the role society expects him to play and because he has discovered that the role is "convenient" in that it allows him a certain freedom to nurse his unconventional thoughts without being questioned. He reveals himself only to the very few who believe what they see, not what they want to see. Defending his contentment with being a servant, Lee says: "'I don't know where being a servant came into disrepute. It is the refuge of the philosopher, the food of the lazy, and, properly carried out, it is a position of power, even of love.'"[37] Samuel also has his "hidey-hole", although it is not quite as necessary nor quite as convenient as Lee's queue and shuffle. He hides behind a mask of Irish joviality: "'I tell jokes because people come all the way to my place to laugh. I try to be funny for them even when the sadness is on me.'"[38] Actually, Samuel is considered rather strange by his neighbors (although he too is respected for his sagacity) because he fails to accept the common standard of economic competition. Samuel finds pleasure in inventing and improving farm machinery, but he is thought a fool because he will not capitalize on his ingenuity, preferring instead to let others benefit from his labors

[36] John Steinbeck, *The Log From the Sea of Cortez* (New York, 1951), p. xlvi.
[37] Steinbeck, *East of Eden*, p. 165.
[38] *Ibid.*, p. 164.

without charge. Like Lee, Samuel thrives on a life of contempla-
tion.

Both men find their religion in the rule of reason. Lee, for
example, is enthralled by the old Chinese and Jewish scholars who,
for two years, study to get at the essence of the Cain-Abel story.
He tells Samuel: "'I went along with them, marveling at the beauty
of their proud clean brains. ... You should have sat through some
of those nights of argument and discussion. The questions, the in-
spection, oh, the lovely thinking — the beautiful thinking.'"[39] And,
quite consistent with the independent thinking of the Steinbeck
hero, neither Lee nor Samuel believes literally that the Old Testament is "'a divine book written by the inky finger of God.'". The
sixteen verses from Genesis are valuable because they tell a true
story, they are "'a history of humankind in any age or culture or
race'".[40] Thus, while they put their faith in rationality, Lee and
Samuel direct their reasoning powers towards determining the
value of the human soul. Their findings, later restated by Samuel,
are best summarized by Lee:

"I feel that a man is a very important thing. ... This is not theology. I
have no bent toward gods. But I have a new love for that glittering
instrument, the human soul. It is a lovely and unique thing in the universe. It is always attacked and never destroyed - because 'Thou
mayest'".[41]

Co-existent with their roles as Steinbeck's heroes, Lee and Samuel
see men and events from a non-teleological point of view. Lee, in
fact, drops his pidgin and admits Samuel into his confidence
because he recognizes that Samuel, like himself, cannot tolerate
illusion and insists upon seeing things as they are: "'You are one
of the rare people who can separate your observation from your
preconception. You see what is, where most people see what they
expect.'"[42] This in itself is Steinbeck's definition of non-teleology,
but *East of Eden* is also the fictional illustration of what Steinbeck
meant when, in *Sea of Cortez*, he declared that only by non-teleo-

---

[39] *Ibid.*, p. 313.
[40] *Ibid.*, pp. 303-304.
[41] *Ibid.*, p. 304.
[42] *Ibid.*, p. 163.

logical methods could man ever really progress. Both Samuel and Lee realize, for example, that intelligent action can be taken by men only after they dispel their illusions. Hence, Lee insists that Caleb face the fact of his guilt in order that he might contend with it. And Samuel shakes Adam from his lethargy, shocks him back into creative life, by forcing him to admit that his illusion of Cathy as a confused innocent is only a distortion of the truth that he has concocted to keep from being hurt. As Samuel puts it, "'I forced him to live or get off the pot.'"[43]

Applied to the novel as a whole, Steinbeck's nonteleological system works this way: It examined in scrupulous detail the human condition under which man is perpetually embroiled in the war between good and evil ("Once a given situation is deeply understood, no apologies are required."[44]) Once this condition is faced and accepted ("the love and understanding of instant acceptance"[45]) then the individual can exercise his power of choice and attempt to rule over sin ("After that fundamental has been achieved, the next step ... can be considered more sensibly."[46])

I have said that *East of Eden* was a passionately moral declaration of Steinbeck's vision of the human condition. Certainly he had often before been concerned with the perpetual struggle in life between the forces of good and evil; but in *East of Eden*, for the first time, Steinbeck went beyond affirming that man is great because he can *survive* that struggle. His vision in this novel is of man victorious over evil. ""Too many of us conceive of a life as ending in defeat,'"[47] says Samuel Hamilton, but if man exercises the power given to him alone to choose between good and evil, that makes him great, "'that gives him stature with the gods'".[48]

[43]. *Ibid.*, p. 309.
[44] John Steinbeck and Edward F. Ricketts, *Sea of Cortez* (New York, 1941), p. 146.
[45] *Ibid.*, p. 147.
[46] *Ibid.*
[47] Steinbeck, *East of Eden*, p. 308.
[48] *Ibid.*, p. 303.

IX

CONCLUSION: THREE NOVELS AND A PRIZE

Steinbeck has written three novels since *East of Eden: Sweet Thursday* (1954), *The Short Reign of Pippin IV* (1957), and *The Winter of Our Discontent* (1961). The first two are mediocre comic diversions; the third, a serious but limited document which dramatizes the decline of public responsibility and individual integrity in mid-twentieth century America. All three are out of the main stream of Steinbeck's thought and art; they are, at least with respect to the development of those major themes which I have attempted to trace, very nearly beside the point of the present study.

Sweet Thursday was expressly intended for conversion to musical comedy; adapted by Rodgers and Hammerstein, and entitled *Pipe Dream*, it did in fact have a successful Broadway run. The book is a sequel to *Cannery Row*, but only in a few superficial ways: the locale is still the wrong side of Monterey's cannery; its inhabitants, with some changes incurred by time and the war, are still Mack and the boys; Doc, with customary wisdom and benevolence, but with far less symbolic purpose, still presides over the show from his headquarters in the Western Biological Laboratories. But there is none of the serious satirical intention of the sort that occasioned *Cannery Row*, no moral purpose other than to produce plenty of musical comedy fun. The plot rests on a predicament no more strenuous than finding Doc a "dame" to kill the "worm of discontent" gnawing at his soul. The book is indeed pleasurable, but only in the restricted sense that made Carlos Baker, in his review for *The New York Times*, recommend it as a "gaily inconsequential" yarn.

The Short Reign of Pippin IV is just as gay as *Sweet Thursday*, and a bit more consequential. *Pippin*, a burlesque of French politics, tries to illustrate how silly a game politics can be when too many people take it too seriously. The hero of the novel, M. Pippin Héristal, is a Chaplinesque little man, an easy-going fellow (his passion is astronomy) who would rather ride his motor scooter than be king. But when the monarchy is restored to France because the dozens of political factions have run out of governments, Pippin, qualified by a trace of royal blood (Charlemagne), is chosen to lead because he is entirely uncontroversial. If the novel has any serious theme underlying its burlesque, it might be found in Pippin's attempt to retain some trace of individuality in the face of a whimsical society. In a novel of such tenuous purpose and form, however, such a theme can bear only the vaguest connection to Steinbeck's earlier interest in the relationship between the individual and the group.

Although *Sweet Thursday* and *Pippin* can hardly be measured against Steinbeck's more ambitious achievements, they do not sadden me as they do some critics who see them as Steinbeck's last literary gasps. Perhaps, in the same sense that Graham Greene uses the term to distinguish his fanciful from his serious work, these novels should be considered "entertainments". As I noted in my introduction, Steinbeck's techniques and subject matter have varied widely and it has thus always been difficult to know what he would be up to next. About this versatility Steinbeck wrote:

Since by the process of writing a book I have outgrown that book, and since I like to write, I have not written two books alike. Where would be the interest in that ... ?

If a writer likes to write, he will find satisfaction in endless experimentation with his medium. He will improvise techniques, arrangements of scenes, rhythms of words, and rhythms of thought. He will constantly investigate and try combinations new to him, sometimes utilizing an old method for a new idea and vice versa. Some of his experiments will inevitably be unsuccessful but he must try them anyway if his interest be alive. This experimentation is not criminal. Perhaps it is not even important, but it is necessary if the writer be not moribund.[1]

Steinbeck had not stopped experimenting and had not stopped being

[1]   John Steinbeck, "Critics, Critics, Burning Bright", *The Saturday Review of Literature*, XXXIII (November 11, 1950), 20-21.

a writer. *The Winter of Our Discontent* is no more like *The Short Reign of Pippin IV* than *Sweet Thursday* is like *East of Eden*.

In *East of Eden*, Samuel Hamilton concluded that man could achieve "stature with the gods" by exercising his right to choose between good and evil. In *The Winter of Our Discontent*, Ethan Allen Hawley, who might have become Samuel's spiritual heir within the pattern of Steinbeck's non-teleological visionaries, appears to forfeit his right and, rather than choosing, glides into the path of evil via the route of cynicism. Steinbeck makes it clear — perhaps too clear — that Ethan and the other blighted characters of the novel are intended to represent the breakdown of hope and the warping of moral vision in America. In a prefatory note, Steinbeck wrote: "Readers seeking to identify the fictional people and places here described would do better to inspect their own communities and search their own hearts, for this book is about a large part of America today."[2] One is tempted to speculate, then, that Steinbeck chose to depart from his thematic pattern, as I have observed it evolving in his "serious" novels, because the new shape of America would not bend to the vital idealism of a Samuel Hamilton, Steinbeck's latest hero. In *The Winter of Our Discontent*, pervasive cynicism has so corrupted the American softened by prosperity, that his will to struggle towards fulfillment of the ideal has been replaced by the illusion that success is sweetest when counted in dollars and power. Steinbeck's dual principle of reality-acceptance fostering progress, cannot function in a world where the individual has lost sight of his moral role in the collective society. *The Winter of Our Discontent*, therefore, depicts, as the title implies, America in a season of corruption and blight, a winter that may perhaps pass but not before it withers a good deal of the nation's soul.

Ethan Hawley is the inheritor — as is America itself — of both the conscience of the past and the corruption of the present. He yields to the latter because he is tired of being poor but honest, and tired of receiving the mocking pity of his family and his townspeople. When he dons the mask of cynicism and goes forth to outplay the town at its own game of "success", he becomes a kind of inverted Steinbeck hero, his counter-heroics illustrating the

[2]   John Steinbeck, *The Winter of Our Discontent* (New York, 1961).

breakdown of Steinbeck's thematic scheme. In the first place, this hero is too cynical too search for gods, albeit he offers sentimental homage to a carved, transluscent stone which he refers to as his "talisman" and keeps locked in a cabinet, a "holy place". Sadly, he relinquishes his right to the talisman and concludes that it rightly belongs to his daughter, within whom the truth-seeking instinct still lives. Secondly, he decides that since the society is corrupt, he might as well work for himself, for "number one". "Temporarily", he rationalizes, "I traded a habit of conduct and attitude for comfort and dignity and a cushion of security."[3] He retreats, as it were, from Steinbeck's dictum that before a man can become himself as an individual, he must be a contributing part of the group. Finally, he is too confused by the chaos of the present to gain the objective distance needed to view events with non-teleological "understanding". He is so muddled by events that, like several of the more pathetic characters of Steinbeck's earlier novels, he seriously considers suicide.

It would not matter, neither to the casual reader nor to the literary critic, that Steinbeck swerved from this or that pattern in his writing; indeed, *The Winter of Our Discontent* is more potent as social criticism because of the shift in pattern. It would not matter that the book is ferociously "moral" — Steinbeck's best works are directed by his moral voice. What disturbs the reader is the failure of the novel to support its moral contentions with believable events and characters. Reviewing the book, Virgilia Peterson summarizes with precision:

Even the sharks themselves could scarcely quarrel with the thesis that today in America honesty is losing its reputation. But it takes more than a thesis to make a novel. No matter how right the author is, how fine his wrath, he will not disturb his readers' sleep or trouble their complacency unless he has filled the arteries of his characters with blood. But how much can we believe in this Ethan who makes such sophisticated jokes when in bed with his Boston-Irish wife and who sees through the maneuvers of one of Steinbeck's least probable huntresses, yet has never heard, till the day we meet him, of the bribe? How far can we believe in a man of innocence and principle who finds it so ridiculously easy to outshark

[3] *Ibid.*, p. 226.

the sharks? And if Ethan himself is hard to accept, the rest of the characters — with the exception of Ethan's wife — are all drawn quite casually
from stock.[4]

. . . .

In 1962, the year after the publication of *The Winter of Our
Discontent*, Steinbeck became the sixth American to receive the
Nobel Prize for Literature for, in the language of the award, "his
realistic and imaginative writings, distinguished as they are by a
sympathetic humor and a social perception". Some critics, in the
mistaken belief that the award was for his latest novel alone,
questioned the choice. Others wondered why the prize had gone to
a writer whose reputation was based on work done nearly a
generation ago. One of these latter, in an article which *The New
York Times* saw fit to publish on the very eve of the Nobel Prize
ceremonies, performed what he referred to as "a fascinating if
somewhat melancholy task" of reviewing the body of Steinbeck's
work and concluding that it was "difficult to find a flattering
explanation for awarding this most distinguished of literary prizes
to a writer whose real but limited talent is, in his best books,
watered down by tenth-rate philosophizing and, in his worst books,
is overwhelmed by it". "Perhaps", speculated the same critic,
"those Europeans who influence the awarding of the prize are
simply behind the times and in all sincerity believe that the judgments of the thirties are still the established judgments".[5]

A spokesman for the Nobel Prize Committee made it clear, however, that the Committee had performed its task after sound literary
consideration and with its usual integrity. *The Winter of Our
Discontent* seemed to have served the Committee most of all as a
reminder of Steinbeck's vast accomplishment; with this novel, it
asserted, Steinbeck had "resumed his position as an independent
expounder of the truth with an unbiased instinct for what is
genuinely American, be it good or wicked". But singled out from
the past was "the towering standard" set by *The Grapes of Wrath*,
the "little masterpiece" *Of Mice and Men*, and the "incomparable"

[4] Virgilia Peterson, "John Steinbeck's Modern Morality Tale", *New York
Herald Tribune Book Review*, June 25, 1961, p. 29.
[5] Arthur Mizener, "Does a Moral Vision of the Thirties Deserve a Nobel
Prize?" *The New York Times Book Review*, December 9, 1962, pp. 4, 44, 45.

collection of short stories, *The Long Valley*. The Committee observed that some critics wished to emphasize signs of Steinbeck's "flagging powers", but it rejected these estimates in preferring to see the whole of his work. Certainly influenced by Steinbeck's humanitarian commitment ("His sympathies always go out to the oppressed, the misfits and the distressed"), the Committee showed that its understanding went beyond that obvious issue: "He likes to contrast the simple joy of life with the brutal and cynical craving for money. But in him we find the American temperament also expressed in his great feeling for nature, for the tilled soil, the wasteland, the mountains and the ocean coasts."[6]

I have commented frequently on Steinbeck's versatility, his craftsmanship in handling a wide range of techniques and subjects which the Nobel Committee recognized as itself a remarkable achievement. But Steinbeck is no mere literary trickster showing off his versatile talent the way a stage magician practices his harmless deceptions. Beneath the surface of these diverse methods is the thematic pattern which has provided a philosophical principle of organization for the body of Steinbeck's novels. Steinbeck accepts the artist's responsibility to create with symbols an ordered universe "in modeled imitation of the observed reality".[7] From his view of man as a physical and spiritual being within a non-causal universe, Steinbeck predicated that man's glory is in being a part of a greater reality:

The whole world is necessarily everything, the whole world of fact and fancy, body and psyche, physical fact and spiritual truth, individual and collective, life and death, macrocosm and microcosm ... conscious and unconscious, subject and object. The whole picture is portrayed by *is*, the deepest word of deep ultimate reality, not shallow or partial as reasons are, but deeper and participating, possibly encompassing the Oriental concept of *being*.[8]

In large part, Steinbeck's novels are the esthetic resolution of these ideas.

[6]   Quoted in *The New York Times*, October 26, 1962, p. 12.
[7]   John Steinbeck and Edward F. Ricketts, *Sea of Cortez* (New York, 1941), p. 2.
[8]   *Ibid.*, pp. 150-151.

BIBLIOGRAPHY

WORKS BY JOHN STEINBECK

A. Books

Cup of Gold (New York, Robert M. McBride & Co., 1929).
The Pastures of Heaven (New York, Brewer, Warren & Putnam, 1932).
To a God Unknown (New York, Robert O. Ballou, 1933).
Tortilla Flat (New York, Covici-Friede, 1935).
In Dubious Battle (New York, Covici-Friede, 1936).
Of Mice and Men (New York, Covici-Friede, 1937).
Of Mice and Men: A Play in Three Acts (New York, Covici-Friede, 1937).
The Long Valley (New York, The Viking Press, 1938).
The Grapes of Wrath (New York, The Viking Press, 1939).
The Forgotten Village (New York, The Viking Press, 1941).
Sea of Cortez (with Edward F. Ricketts) (New York, The Viking Press, 1941).
The Moon is Down (New York, The Viking Press, 1942).
The Moon is Down: A Play in Two Parts (New York, Dramatists Play Service, Inc., 1942).
Bombs Away (New York, The Viking Press, 1942).
The Red Pony (New York, The Viking Press, 1945).
Cannery Row (New York, The Viking Press, 1945).
The Pearl (New York, The Viking Press, 1947).
The Wayward Bus (New York, The Viking Press, 1947).
A Russian Journal (with photographs by Robert Capa) (New York, The Viking Press, 1948).
Burning Bright (New York, The Viking Press, 1950).
The Log From the Sea of Cortez (New York, The Viking Press, 1951).
East of Eden (New York, The Viking Press, 1952).
Sweet Thursday (New York, The Viking Press, 1954).
The Short Reign of Pippin IV (New York, The Viking Press, 1957).
Once There Was a War (New York, The Viking Press, 1958).
The Winter of Our Discontent (New York, The Viking Press, 1961).
Travels With Charley (New York, Curtis Publishing Co., 1961).

B. *Selected Articles, Essays, and Letters*

"Dubious Battle in California", *The Nation*, CXII (September 12, 1936), 302-304.

"The Way It Seems to John Steinbeck", *Occident*, Fall, 1936, p. 5.

Dispatches from the European War Theater. *New York Herald Tribune*, June 21 — December 10, 1943.

"Over There", *Ladies Home Journal*, LXI (February, 1944).

"The G.I.'s War ...", *New York Herald Tribune Weekly Book Review*, May 18, 1947, p.1. A review of *Yank*.

Introduction, *Between Pacific Tides* (rev. ed.), Edward F. Ricketts and Jack Calvin (Stanford, Stanford University Press, 1948).

"Miracle of Tepazac", *Colliers*, CXII (December 25, 1948) 22-23.

"Critics, Critics, Burning Bright", *Saturday Review of Literature*, XXXIII (November 11, 1950), 20-21.

"The Secret Weapon We Were Afraid to Use", *Colliers*, CXXXI (January 10, 1953), 9-13.

"My Short Novels", *Wings*, October, 1953, pp. 1-8.

"A Letter on Criticism", *Colorado Quarterly*, IV (Autumn, 1955).

"How to Tell Good Guys from Bad Guys", *The Reporter*, XII (March 10, 1955), 42-44.

"Some Thoughts on Juvenile Delinquency", *The Saturday Review*, XXXVIII (May 28, 1955), 22.

"Critics from a Writer's Point of View", *Saturday Review*, XXXVIII (August 27, 1955), 20.

"Joan in All of Us", *Saturday Review*, XXXIX (January 14, 1956), 17.

"My War With the Ospreys", *Holiday*, XXI (March, 1957), 72-73, 163-165.

"Game of Hospitality", *Saturday Review*, XL (April 20, 1957), 24.

Letter to Adlai Stevenson, in *The Toledo Blade*. March 13, 1960, Sec. 6, p. 1. Expressing concern over the moral state of the nation.

Letter to Adlai Stevenson, in *The Toledo Blade*. March 27, 1960, Sec. 6, p.. 1. More on the subject of the nation's moral weaknesses.

"America and the Americans", *The Saturday Evening Post*, July 2, 1966, pp. 33-38, 40, 41, 44, 46, 47.

SELECTED CRITICISM

"Assisting John Steinbeck", *Newsweek*, XLVII (June, 1956), 56.

Baker, Carlos, "*In Dubious Battle* Revalued", *New York Times Book Review*, July 25, 1943, pp. 4, 16.

——, "Steinbeck of California", *Delphian Quarterly*, XXIII (April, 1940), 40-45.

Beach, Joseph Warren, *American Fiction, 1920-1940* (New York, Macmillan, 1941).

Bowron, Bernard, "*The Grapes of Wrath*: A 'Wagons West' Romance", *Colorado Quarterly*, III (Summer, 1954), 84-91.

Boynton, Percy H., "John Steinbeck", *Americans in Contemporary Fiction* (Chicago, 1940), pp. 241-257.

Bracher, Frederick, "Steinbeck and the Biological View of Man", *Pacific Spectator*, II (Winter, 1948), 14-29.

Brustein, Robert, "America's New Culture Hero: Feelings Without Words", *Commentary*, XXV (February, 1958), 123-129.

Burgum, Edwin B., "The Sensibility of John Steinbeck", *Science and Society*, X (1946), 132-147.

Calverton, V. F., "Steinbeck, Hemingway and Faulkner", *Modern Quarterly*, XI (Fall, 1939), 36-44.

Cannon, Gerard, "The Pauline Apostleship of Tom Joad", *College English*, XXIV (December, 1962), 222-224.

Carpenter, Frederick I., "John Steinbeck: American Dreamer", *Southwest Review*, XXVI (July, 1941), 454-467.

——, "The Philosophical Joads", *College English*, II (1941), 315-325.

Champney, Freeman, "John Steinbeck, Californian", *Antioch Review*, VII (Fall, 1947), 345-362.

Charvat, William, "American Romanticism and the Depression of 1937", *Science and Society*, II (Winter, 1937), 67-82.

Commager, Henry S., *The American Mind* (New Haven, Yale University Press, 1954).

Cousins, Norman, "Bankrupt Realism", *Saturday Review*, XXX (March 8, 1947), 22-23.

Cowley, Malcom, "New Tendencies in the Novel: Pure Fiction", *New Republic*, CXXI (November 28, 1949), 32-35.

——, "'Not Men': A Natural History of American Naturalism", *Kenyon Review*, IX (Spring, 1947), 414-435.

Crockett, H. Kelley, "The Bible and *The Grapes of Wrath*", *College English*, XXIV (December, 1962), 193-199.

Danford, Merle, "A Critical Survey of John Steinbeck: His Life and the Development of His Writings", unpublished Master's thesis, English Department, Ohio University, 1939.

Davis, Elmer, "The Steinbeck Country", *Saturday Review*, XVIII (September 24, 1938), 11.

Dean, Leonard, Introduction to Erasmus' *The Praise of Folly* (New York, Farrar, Straus, 1946).

Dunn, Thomas F., "*The Grapes of Wrath*", *College English*, XXIV (April, 1963), 566-567.

Dougherty, Charles T., "The Christ Figure in *The Grapes of Wrath*", *College English*, XXIV (December, 1962), 224-226.

Embler, Weller, "Metaphor and Social Belief", *ETC.*, VIII (Winter, 1951).

Fairley, Barker, "John Steinbeck and the Coming Literature", *Sewanee Review*, L (April, 1942), 145-161.

Farrell, James T., "Social Themes in American Realism", *English Journal*, XXXV (June, 1946), 309-314.

——, "Some Observations on Naturalism, So Called, in American Fiction", *Antioch Review*, X (Summer, 1950), 247-264.

Freel, Eugene L., "A Comparative Study Between Certain Concepts and Principles of Modern Psychology and the Writings of John Steinbeck", unpublished Ph. D. dissertation, New York University, 1947.

French, Warren G., "Another Look at *The Grapes of Wrath*", *Colorado Quarterly*, III (Winter, 1955), 337-343.

——, *John Steinbeck* (New York, Twayne, 1961).

Freud, Sigmund, *Moses and Monotheism*, tr. by Katherine Jones (New York, Alfred A. Knopf, Inc., 1939).

Frohock, W. M., "John Steinbeck's Men of Wrath", *Southwest Review*, XXXI (Spring, 1946), 144-152.

——, *The Novel of Violence in America, 1920-1950* (Dallas, Southern Methodist University Press, 1950).

Gannett, Lewis, "John Steinbeck's Way of Writing", the Introduction to *The Portable Steinbeck*. New York, The Viking Press, 1946.

——, "John Steinbeck: Novelist at Work", *Atlantic Monthly*, CLXXVI (December, 1945), 55-61.

Geismar, Maxwell, "John Steinbeck: Of Wrath or Joy", *Writers in Crisis*. Boston, 1942, pp. 237-270.

Gibbs, Lincoln R., "John Steinbeck, Moralist", *Antioch Review*, II (1942), 172-184.

Gierasch, Walter, "Steinbeck's *The Red Pony*, II, 'The Great Mountains'", *Explicator*, IV (March, 1946), 39.

Goldsmith, Arnold, "Thematic Rhythm in *The Red Pony*", *College English*, XXVI (February, 1965), 391-394.

Graves, Robert, Introduction to *The Golden Ass of Apuleius* (New York, Farrar, Straus and Young, Inc., 1951).

Hoffman, Frederick J., *Freudianism and the Literary Mind* (Baton Rouge, Louisiana State University Press, 1945).

——, *The Modern Novel in America* (Chicago, Henry Regnery Co., 1951).

Hyman, Stanley E., "John Steinbeck and the Nobel Prize", *New Leader*, XLV (December 10, 1962), 10-11.

——, "Some Notes on John Steinbeck", *Antioch Review*, II (1942), 185-200.

Jones, Claude E., "Proletarian Writing and John Steinbeck", *Sewanee Review*, XLVIII (1940), 445-456.

Jung, Carl G., *Modern Man in Search of a Soul*. Tr. W. S. Dill and Cary F. Baynes (New York, Harcourt, Brace and Co., 1933).

Kale, Bernard, "The Author", *Saturday Review*, XXXV (September 20, 1952), 11.

Kazin, Alfred, "The Unhappy Man From Happy Valley", *The New York Times Book Review*, May 4, 1958, pp. 1, 29.

Krutch, Joseph Wood, "John Steinbeck's Dramatic Tale of Three Generations", *New York Herald Tribune Book Review*, September 21, 1952, p. 1.

Lisca, Peter, "*The Grapes of Wrath* as Fiction, *PMLA*, LXXXII (March, 1957), 296-309.

——, "Motif and Pattern in *Of Mice and Men*", *Modern Fiction Studies*, II (Winter, 1956-57), 228-234.

——, *The Wide World of John Steinbeck* (New Brunswick, Rutgers University Press, 1958).

Magny, Claude-Edmonde, "*East of Eden*", *Perspectives, USA*, V (Fall, 1953), 146-152.

Metzger, Charles, "Steinbeck's Version of the Pastoral", *Modern Fiction Studies* (Summer, 1960), pp. 115-124.

Mizener, Arthur, "Does a Moral Vision of the Thirties Deserve a Nobel Prize?" *The New York Times Book Review*, December 9, 1962, pp. 4, 44, 45.

Moore, Harry T., *The Novels of John Steinbeck: A First Critical Study* (Chicago, 1939).

——, "Steinbeck the Soft-Hearted Satirist", *New Republic*, CXXXVI (May 27, 1957), 23-24.

Moore, Ward, "*Cannery Row* Revisited: Steinbeck and the Sardine", *Nation*, CLXXIX (October 16, 1954) 325-327.

Mosier, Richard D., *The American Temper: Pattern of Our Intellectual Heritage* (California, 1952).

Nevius, Blake, "Steinbeck: One Aspect", *Pacific Spectator*, III (Summer, 1949), 302-311.

Nichols, Lewis, "A Talk With John Steinbeck", *New York Times Book Review*, September 28, 1952, p. 30.

Peterson, Virgilia, "John Steinbeck's Modern Morality Tale", *New York Herald Tribune Book Review*, June 25, 1961, p. 29.

Phillips, William, "Male-ism and Moralism", *American Mercury*, LXXV (October, 1952), 93-98.

Rascoe, Burton, "John Steinbeck", *English Journal*, XXVII (1938), 205-216.

Reik, Theodor, *The Psychological Problems of Religion-Ritual*. Tr. Douglas Bryan (New York, Farrar, Straus and Company, 1946).

Ross, Woodburn O., "John Steinbeck: Earth and Stars", *University of Missouri Studies*, XXI (1946), 177-179.

——, "John Steinbeck: Naturalism's Priest", *College English*, X (May, 1949), 432-437.

Santayana, George, *The Life of Reason*, rev. ed. (New York, Charles Scribner's Sons, 1955).

Shedd, Margaret, "*Of Mice and Men*", *Theatre Arts*, XVII (October, 1937), 774-780.

Shockley, Martin S., "The Reception of *The Grapes of Wrath* in Oklahoma", *American Literature*, XV (January, 1944), 351-361.

——, "Christian Symbolism in *The Grapes of Wrath*", *College English*, XVII (November, 1956), 87-90.

Sinnott, Edmund W., *The Biology of the Spirit* (New York, The Viking Press, 1955).

Tarr, E. W., "Steinbeck on One Plane", *Saturday Review*, XXX (December 20, 1947), 20.

Taylor, Walter F., "*The Grapes of Wrath* Reconsidered", *Mississippi Quarterly*, XII (Summer, 1959), 136-144.

Tedlock, E. W. and C. V. Wicker, ed., *Steinbeck and His Critics* (Albuquerque, University of New Mexico Press, 1957).

Whipple, T. K., "Steinbeck Through a Glass, Though Brightly", *New Republic*, XLIV (October 12, 1938), 274-275.

Wilson, Edmund, "The Californians: Storm and Steinbeck", *New Republic*, CIII (December 9, 1940), 784-787.

——, *The Boys in the Back Room* (San Francisco, Colt Press, 1941).

Wright, Celeste T., "Ancient Analogues of an Incident in John Steinbeck", *Western Fiction* January, 1955, pp. 50-51.

INDEX